Stanislav Bachev

—

Parameters of the Post-American World Order

Published by

Amazon KDP

USA

2021

About the author

Stanislav Bachev is a Bulgarian political analyst, a historian and a public figure. He has a PhD in Political Science. He is a published and solicited author in Bulgaria and Russia. "Parameters of the Post-American world order" is first published in Bulgaria in 2020 by one of the three biggest publishing houses. In 2021 it is published in Russia by the International Writers Union.

Personal website: http://bachev.bg

Amazon, Kindle, and Fire and all related logos are trademarks of Amazon.com, Inc. or its affiliates.

Contents

STANISLAV BACHEV

Preface

The task of setting and predetermining the direction of global relations development requires the collection, analysis and comprehension of a vast amount of information over a long period of time. Even trying to look forward, beyond today and now, would be perceived as, at best, intellectual immodesty. Every piece of work that comes out from under the author's pen is a reflection of his vision of the world. However, the present text attempts to look beyond one's own desires, building on the realistic basis of the present and past facts to create a projection of the future. It means that the general categorisation framework for emotional favouring of one or another great power is narrow and therefore inapplicable. Although history is primarily an emotion, the realistic-possible does not follow the emotion, but this is not a purely historical text, and its claim does not head in this direction. On the contrary, the task is difficult enough to claim the current attempt at exhaustiveness of facts and examples, but rather the goal is to create models. The book's appearance occurs amid the viral pandemic spread in 2020 that showed the consumer age's weaknesses and vices. It pointed out the countries that turned out to be unprepared in every field and societies whose reflexes are being subjected to tests and trials. The information environment has proven its huge impact on the societies and emotions that can be created in them. On a large scale, people find themselves in a closed circle they have made themselves. On one side is the frantic masochistic desire to satisfy their information hunger, a reflection of one's life. On the other side is the temptation that lurks everywhere – endless streams of information offering to satisfy the need for fear, panic and uncriticism. It is probably the beautiful, cheerful irony in the unplanned release of this book – the need for a clear, reasonable, and positive look ahead. The world was on the threshold of a new time, with processes taking place over the last two decades and setting the methodological signs of the coming change. The 2020 crisis turned out to be the appropriate catharsis, which first highlighted the system's actual problems, and secondly – opened up opportunities for a new beginning.

A one-sided view of the world is not possible – only from the point of view of strict reason and logic. Time shows that the most outstanding achievements are firstborn of an emotional impulse of passion, falling in love with an idea and burning in it. Subsequently, the mind and science chart the path. For us, the contemporaries of events, time may seem like infinity, when we are stray and with a view close to dealing with each day, as defeating one enemy by the end of the week and month; or it runs relentlessly when we are busy and miss the daily beauty around us – like the leafing of a spring tree, which follows its methodical course, realising its own perseverance. This same time for history is just a moment, a speck of dust that has fallen on the forgotten books in the great library. However, the advantage of people is that they can choose and see all the beauty at once – as long as they want. We can be at the height of history when it is necessary to weigh every process that happens around us reasonably. Still, we can also estimate the lasting of a single minute in which a whole whirlwind of emotions can be accommodated. And it is what makes us humans – the ability and instinct to gaze at the future, yet, the hands to feel every detail of the present and past.

Introduction

Analysing the processes in the world, placing them within a model, and explaining them cannot happen without returning to history. Understanding the present means understanding the past and designing the future results from a synthesis between the two. To trace the relations between countries, with their peculiarities and even emotion, is, in fact, to consider interpersonal relations. Each country is a many times magnified model of human as a set of positive and negative traits. That is why the transposition of human traits on states and international relations is not only necessary but obligatory to capture their character objectively. Emotions such as a sense of truth, justice, a sense of memory, reflexes in a state of threat or crisis are characteristic of us as people and societies and on a larger international level. The memory of a person determines their life and goals; the memory of a family preserves the sense of lineage and values. And they, in turn, create a collective sense of community that builds a state. And the successful organisation of larger communities or unions depends only on the historical maturity of the states and the overcoming, but not forgetting, of the old problems and contradictions. It means that the idea of forgetting and blurring the national, for the more minor forms of community, in the name of some common dream goal is absolutely wrong and would only lead to the distortion of history, hence to the distortion of the future. Firstly, because of repeating old mistakes and secondly, because of the possibility of destroying the collective and individual soul mentality. Only by preserving their memory, sense of nation, and nationality a group of states can exist within a healthy union based on a pragmatic foundation and a conscious cultural closeness and tolerance.

In recent years, a purposeful process has been underway in Europe in an attempt to blur, distort and replace the collective memory in order to create enemies on a psychological and cultural level – a much more dangerous process than purely economic opposition because it will be passed on to the next generation if it succeeds. Creating enemies – both physical and invisible (real and fake) – means entering the individual, and then entire societies, into a state of fear, which means first encapsulating and then falling into a state of helplessness. Because fear, if not overcome, will lead to individual and collective suspicion, a manifestation of aggression both inward and outward and ultimately to a state of disintegration – in man spiritually and physically, and in the state or union of the social contract. From the state's point of view, the condition of fear instilled in one's people and the long-term cultivation of an enemy figure means an unconscious social renunciation of the feeling of spiritual freedom and personal space, with the only promise of physical protection. War creates the state, and the state continues the feeling of a state of war in an infinite algorithm to rationalise its own superpowers.

In recent decades, the world has been in a state of gradual and irreversible change. It means that the imposed model experiment for a unipolar world, which began with the end of the Cold War, failed. The world we live in has known many oppositions over the years: civilisation – barbarism; Christianity – paganism; democracy – communism; West-East, etc., but for the first time a confrontation of a new type: the United States – almost all others, managed to mature and acquire a general character in this new time. Because of its unprecedented influence and unprecedented thirst for resources and capital, one country managed to achieve something that no one else has achieved – it managed to gain the contempt and suspicion of all. This outcome happened consistently, not as a one-time event but was unfolded over many years. The discourse on the idea of a post-American world order necessarily means that there was a world order which by its nature and characteristics can be called American. With a global influence and scope that has never been seen before. History gives once such a chance, and the one that the United States gained at the end of the Cold War was successfully lost and failed for a number of reasons. The condition of historical immaturity and lack of creative instinct is one of the root causes of ignorance of how to use such an exclusive responsibility – to be the first and only hegemon on the planet. The state of Europe as instincts, reflexes and perception of the world results from development and turbulent processes over a period of over 2000 years, while in the United States, this historical experience is missing. Historical youth and the highly explosive attainment of a condition of world influence deprive the state and its elite of time to comprehend the lessons of history. The lack of a global war on its continental territory affects perceptions and creates an inability to withstand the sight of the catastrophe of war. The lack of such experience and the arrogant self-declaration of exceptionalism are the reasons for not realising the need for a welfare and social state. Following the example of the one we see built in Western Europe or the Scandinavian countries. Their internal issues – from public and social to administrative provoke external manifestations of force by causing instability and chaos and creating conflict zones around the world. The growth of the

United States to a world hegemon is entirely related to a condition in which the internal content does not correspond to the external form. The lack of spiritual readiness of one's society and the difference in the elite's attitude, through the adopted idea of the universal empire in its western branch, naturally lead in the long run to problems that ultimately mean an early state of decline. The early plucked green fruit is also unable to ripen properly. Despite the condition of decline, the influence of the Giant by its nature still remains global and is inevitably part of any new model of regulating international relations.

Against this background, over the last 10 years, the world has witnessed how a country has managed to rise from the dead and rediscover itself so that it can become a factor without which no global problem can be solved. Russia, the direct successor and representative of the eastern branch of the universal empire idea, managed to emerge from the timelessness after the end of the Cold War, to adapt and show in practice that a crisis that fails to break the tree makes it stronger. The key lies in the metaphor of the tree, which draws its strength from the strong roots of the past, but uses historical time correctly to be able to spread its branches higher.

The third country that participated in forming the post-American world order is the bearer of a millennial culture and has also resurrected, but even from an even longer period of oppression and exploitation by the so-called Western, civilised world. China has managed to overcome the "workshop of the world" stereotype but started by helping to buy and trade global influence. And it is already demonstrating, without being intrusive, its own socio-cultural model as an alternative.

Discipline, shared energy and purpose, the vast market, and gigantic scope and scale of action in all directions have created the conditions for the Chinese state to be at the heart of the new security architecture in the world.

The three countries form a security model that takes the form of a three-dimensional triangular prism, in which the base of the three is most important for world order and stability. According to their regional or local influence, the roles of the European Union, Israel, India, Iran, Turkey, Saudi Arabia, and other actors are distributed in the following levels of the prism. Changes in the world are inevitable, and the processes of the last two decades have proved to be the final preparatory action. The irony of the story is that a new but at the same time old factor will strike a decisive blow at the status quo. The emergence of the viral pandemic in 2020, whether as a natural process of the micro world to bring balance to the earth or as a social and scientific-information experiment, still managed to test the reflexes and instincts of all countries and societies. It assigns the 2020 pandemic the role of a catalyst for international relations entering into a new stage. The strength of the media environment has created a state of trance and anaesthesia in world societies, which has made the pandemic suitable "murky water", allowing the world's processes to continue their course without resistance. The debate on the inevitable need to revive a strong nation-state, which is able to cope alone in times of crisis, also received an unequivocal answer. The successful adaptation of the countries that, even before the 2020 crisis, participated in the paradigm shift processes in international relations means their secure participation at the heart of the new security architecture. For smaller countries, the harsh lesson remains that accountability to one's people means rethinking and changing stateless policies in the strategic sectors of the economy. It, in turn, is linked to the restoration of a strong education system, which is a prerequisite for building a society prepared for any challenge. Any financial crisis, natural disaster or social experiment ultimately has a positive side, showing the shortcomings of a system and the ability to correct them.

The basis of the present work is to trace the rise of an empire, its impact on the world both at the economy and military power level, but especially at the level of culture, language and spirituality – as a country's true heritage and merit of its majesty and greatness. The strength of the sword and the size of the armies proved to be a transitional but obligatory element in building state power. Lack of historical experience, arrogance and a sense of exclusivity, but also a lack of adaptation are the factors that predetermine the empire's decline. The study's primary focus is the formation of new post-American world order and the opportunities for states and alliances. This also determines the analysis' temporal boundaries of – the end of the 19th, the whole of the 20th and the challenges of the 21st century.

1

Genesis and Parameters of the American World Order

§ 1. The boiling cauldron for melting nations

> *"Here he stands, the great Melting Cauldron - listen! Can't you hear the roar and the bubbling? There gapes his mouth - the port where thousands come from the corners of the earth, along with their burden. Ah, what stirring and boiling! Celts and Latins, Slavs and Teutons, Greeks and Syrians ..."*[1]

The time from the end of the 19th and the beginning of the 20th century passes under the strong influence of industrialisation, rapid globalisation and the establishment of nationalism in the politics of states. International relations in the world are still subject to the influence of the European Great Powers. From the beginning of the 19th to the beginning of the 20th century, Europeans occupied 85% of the earth's territory. In the 1880s, the partition of Africa occurred, and then China was divided into spheres of influence. The longest period of peace in Europe until then, which began in 1815 with the end of the Napoleonic Wars and the formation of the so-called European

---

[1] Excerpt from the play "The Melting Pot" by Israel Zangwill of 1908 - author's note

concert, disrupted only by relatively short wars, heralded a storm. Talking about peace reached its peak in 1901 when the first Nobel Peace Prize was awarded and confirmed the axiom that the more something is talked about, the more it is not done. In the shadow of peace, the coming Great War is systematically planned. Europe is divided into blocs through a series of agreements. This novelty in European relations – to build peacetime defence alliances – shows the inevitability of the clash. First, the Austro-German Union was formed, signed in 1879, to which Italy joined, and then the Franco-Russian Treaty of 1894.

At the same time, after Bismarck came down from power in 1890, German interest in world politics and appetite for acquiring colonies began. Although late, against the background of other European countries, entering the race for territories of the already established and powerful German state caused fear and paranoia. Colonial rivalry worldwide and the struggle for raw materials on the idea of self-sufficiency of the state are becoming additional significant reasons for the fragile peace violation.

At the same time, in the West, across the Atlantic, processes are underway that will lead to an explosion and then; as a result, the birth of new great power. The growth of the United States to world power is an objective regularity, resulting from several factors.

The Declaration of Independence of 1776, the adoption of the Constitution in 1789 and The US Bill of Rights, which comprises the first ten amendments to the Constitution, become the solid foundation that the state needs in its validation. The three documents become a kind of civil religion, bringing the state, its interests and the rights of its citizens to a sacred level, standing above the level of daily politics, that is, excluding the possibility of mistakes and corruption. The sacred significance of the founding documents is unequivocally demonstrated through the way they are stored and not just because of the peculiarities related to the physical preservation of their condition. The rotunda of the US National Archives is much closer in feel to a temple than to the traditional understanding of a museum or archive.[2] A temple that poetises and gives meaning to all the future imperial ambitions of a country. If Protestantism as an inward-looking denomination is at the heart of the capitalist and industrial rise of the United States then the cult of the state is the key to understanding the future approach to the outside world.

Another factor that predetermines the regularity of US growth into a world power is the territorial expansion on the continent. Taking advantage of the wars in Europe and the need for money, the United States bought the vast Louisiana region from Napoleon for $ 15 million in 1803, and in 1819 received Florida for $5 million from Spain. The further expansion to the southwest on the road to complete unification was a slower process. For a period of almost 10 years, between 1836 and 1845, the Texas region, inhabited by American colonists, then The Lone Star Republic was

---

[2]The first vault in which the three basic documents are kept was built in 1953. from Molster Safe Company. It weighs 55 tons and is the size of an ordinary wardrobe only. It is built with humidity, temperature control, resistant to nuclear explosion. It is built with a lifting mechanism that retracts the sarcophagus in the evening. At the beginning of the 21st century, $ 110 million was invested in the complete renovation of the safe. The details of the project are secret. - author's note

at war with Mexico, of which it was part to join the United States.[3] With the Guadalupe Treaty, the United States received from Mexico the territories of present-day Texas, New Mexico, California, Nevada, Utah, Arizona, Oklahoma, Kansas, Colorado, and Wyoming. It is a vast territory shaping the entire American southwest and even north through the state of Wyoming. In 1846 the dispute with Great Britain over the territory of Oregon was resolved, and the border with Canada was established along the 49th parallel. The successful conquest of the Atlantic and Pacific territories is an excellent precondition for future economic and political progress, both in terms of raw materials, a place to live a fulfilling life, attractive to European and Asian immigrants, which will create the finished image of the American nation.

In the run-up to "The boiling cauldron for melting of nations" period, Americans were predominantly British, their language - English, and religiously, as already mentioned, Protestantism occupied a large part of the moral and working world of the young nation. The great challenge facing the state is the different economic and moral character between the North and the South. The clash between the capitalist, industrialising North and the plantation, slave-owning South becomes inevitable. The North has established stable relations with the western part of the country, where there are producers of grain and corn, taking advantage of the then-new technologies of land cultivation and production. But also the severance of the logistical connection with the South on the Mississippi and its replacement with the

---

built canals of the North. The Civil War of 1861-1865 shows the exceptional superiority of the industrial capitalist order over the slave-owning plantation system. The difference in the speed and quality of arms and goods production, the logistical connectivity and the human factor, in general, are crucial to the Union's victory. The Civil War consolidates the young nation, clears the doubts about the correctness of the capitalist path and opens all possibilities for what will then seem like a bright dream for all countries of the world that will be eager to get into the boiling cauldron to be melted into the common American nation. It is important to note that what is sacrificed for this union is a challenging detail but also neglected so much. The West and territory of the central states are under control, and the frontier is gone. Nor is the authentic American culture developed over 300 years – that of the Native Americans, the Indians. The continent is joined at the cost of a lot of blood and the erasure of a unique and genuinely different world from Europe. The Indian Wars ended in 1891 with the defeat of the Sioux at Wounded Knee. Until the beginning of the new century, the Indians were interned in reserves, their culture – broken forever. This grim example from the just-begun history of the young state shows too much about the attitude of future Americans toward everything external and different. The attempt to break with European roots, but at the same time to transpose the imperial line from antiquity, has one of the worst features of the so-called "civilisation". The misunderstanding of the "Other" makes him a barbarian, uncivilised, who must be affiliated, regardless of the means. The lack of understanding, or more precisely even the lack of experience in understanding the different cultures, calls for one's own barbaric instincts to eliminate what cannot be understood.

Eventually, the new state, claiming a new approach that brings together and unites diversity, begins its journey to the future with the same vices it has tried to escape.

Here it is the place to note precisely this consciously made connection with the past. Continuity with antiquity, first logically and naturally borrowed from the British Empire, and then the distinction made with the British beginning and the construction of a bridge between Ancient Rome and the new American state. In its western version, the idea of the Third Rome has been restored and applied in almost every state's aspect – from the concept of the republican beginning, through the legal basis, and in the purely material world – the manifestation in architecture etc. Any empire that claims exclusivity and global expression of its influence parallels the past and, in particular, the Roman Empire. The Eastern manifestation goes through building a connection with the Eastern Roman Empire – Byzantium, which is the direct descendant and successor of the Roman Empire. The model of imperial continuity, giving sacredness to the state and its interests, has been transposed to Bulgaria since the time of Tsar Simeon and his imperial program, called by Prof. Iv. Bozhilov– *pax Symeonica*[4], and then to Russia. Throughout all stages of history,

---

[4] Prof. Ivan Bozhilov defined the imperial idea of Tsar Simeon as follows: community - pax Symeonica. "- Iv. Bozhilov, V. Mutafchieva, K. Kosev, A. Pantev, S. Grancharov. History of Bulgaria.
Prof. Ivan Bozhilov adds that the perimeter of this idea is initially limited in nature - first it is aimed at the elite of society, then to inspire confidence in all Bulgarians. We see the same pattern today in Russia - Vladimir Putin's rhetoric and actions are already aimed at all Russians, he has repeatedly spoken in his speeches about raising Russian self-confidence,

the idea of a new order has acquired names according to which country is trying to achieve its universal presence – from the original source, *pax Romana*, through *Pax Britannica*, etc. It is no coincidence that in the 20th century, the term *pax Americana* became popular, referring to the same universalist meaning. The American state became the bearer of the Western branch of the idea of Third Rome. Historically, Napoleon Bonaparte made a similar transfer of imperial sacredness, seeing himself as a Roman emperor and Paris as the new Rome. The words attributed to him, *"I am a true Roman Emperor, I am of the best lineage of the Caesars - those who are creators."* confirm the principle of *translation imperii*. For example, in the Eastern branch, there are similar personal examples. Like the seal of Tsar Simeon of Bulgaria, which reads *"Simeon Basileus Mirotvorets – many summers"*[5] (Симеон Василевс Миротворец – многая лета). The phrase "Mirotvorets" consists of two words – *мир and творец*. The literal translation of the first word is "peace", but it is not the meaning used in the phrase. The used meaning comes form the old Bulgarian Cyrillic word *миръ*, which means *"world"*, which is still in use. The second word is

---

Russian pride and the equality of the Russian people with everyone else. In order to implement such a program (if we avoid the words doctrine and ideology) it takes time - the changes are like seeds sown on fertile soil, they must happen not only externally, as happens in Bulgaria in the time of Simeon, but also internally - in the soul of people and, above all, economically sustainable preconditions. For the second part, Simeon's time is not enough - the great resource accumulated before and during his reign was lost, followed by a crisis in combination with other factors. What survives the crisis and the economic inadequacy of ambition is the spiritual energy, which, in fact, is the greatness of Simeon - author's note
[5] See History of Bulgaria, Ivan Bozhilov, Vera Mutafchieva, Konstantin Kosev, Andrey Pantev, Stoycho Grancharov, p. 57.

творец, which translates as *"creator"*. This way the phrase becomes *"creator of a new world"*. After the Ottoman conquest of Constantinople in 1453, Sultan Mehmed 2 Fatih called himself *Kayser-i Rum*, literally translated *Roman Caesar*. And in the 16th century, the Russian Monk Philotheus wrote a letter to the Grand Duke Vasily 3 Ivanovich, which contained the phrase "*... because two Romes have fallen, the Third stands, and a Fourth shall never be.*" This way, the idea of Moscow as the Third and Last Rome is being built to this day.

The transfer of the idea of a universal empire to the United States is a natural consequence, spread by the European Enlightenment in the new state and lay with the creation of the Constitution. What distinguishes the new American system is the perception of the republican principle, unlike the previous Universalist models, which are based on the monarchical model of representation. Consideration of the American social model can acquire a complete form and meaning when one steps on certain points of reference that outline both the external silhouette and form and the internal specifics, features, and even shortcomings.

At the very end of the 19th century, united and consolidated as a state, America began to attract like a magnet foreigners from all over the world, seeking new fulfilment and new life. This strange syncretism of nations, if not incorporated into a common model, will not allow the collection of the necessary energy, which we later see as an explosion of the economy, and subsequently, the external manifestation at the political level. To properly understand why a common state, distinctive model is needed, one should look at the statistics of migrant flows entering the United States and their enormous, critical impact on creating the future world empire.

It is no coincidence that the chapter begins with a quote from the play "The Melting Pot" by the English playwright of Jewish origin, Israel Zangwill. Because American society is migrant in nature, every American can trace their roots to Europe, Asia, Africa, and other continents, except for a very small percentage of indigenous people. For example, in 1822, shortly after the start of official statistics, the number of immigrants who entered the United States was 6,911.[6] For 1842 the number is already 104,565 to be able to make another giant leap, just 12 years later – almost half a million in 1854 and nearly 800,000 in 1882. Thus, forthee1850-1900period, nearly 17 million people entered the country, who subsequently built their families, grow and shape the new nation and new big cities such as New York, Chicago or the German diaspora in the Central and Western states. The second big wave, twice as big as the first one, only for a period of 24 years, between 1901 and 1925, 16 million people entered the United States legally, equal to the entire previous 50-year period. A curious and not so positive feature is the Chinese exclusion, provoked after the Gold Rush in California and the first wave of Chinese immigrants. Congress passed several laws that, along with the Chinese Exclusion Act of 1882, banned Chinese migration to the United States until its abolition in 1943. This Chinese wave of settlers

---

[6]Migration Policy Institute, U.S. Immigration trends
https://www.migrationpolicy.org/programs/data-hub/us-immigration-trends#history

forms the Chinese cities so characteristic of the United States and is widely used as a curious feature in the film industry, as neighbourhoods of large cities.

The American professor David Traxel wrote his book *"1898: The Birth of the American Century"*, emphasising the key and fundamental role of New York in the whole of American society and the subsequent export of American influence around the world. Traxel used the year 1898 as a key year, as it marked the official consolidation of the smaller municipalities of Brooklyn, Queens, Manhattan, the Bronx and Staten Island into the nowadays large metropolis of New York. The city is growing, as Traxel writes, from 39 square miles (about 100 square kilometres) to 320 (about 800 square kilometres). In one night, the city became the second largest in the world after London. A good description of the spirit of change and citizens can be found in the same book: *"New Yorkers who voted to create this giant city in a referendum were convinced that soon will surpass London; they were already proud that New York had twice as many phones."*[7]

New York is a suitable and accurate example even in terms of the population and its percentage for the whole country. For example, around 1920, the population of the entire state of Nevada, which, despite its mostly desert nature, is larger in area than countries such as Romania or almost three times that of Bulgaria, has a population of 80,000. Nevada is not the only example. Many of the central states still have a huge contrast, both

---

[7]David Traxel, 1898: The Birth of the American Century, p. 12

in quality of life and population, with the states of the East and West Coasts. By 1920 New York City alone, excluding the metropolis, had a larger population than Mississippi, Montana, Nebraska, Nevada, New Mexico, Rhode Island, and South Dakota taken together. Within ten years, from 1850 to 1860,it doubled from 696,000 to almost 1.2 million. And just ten years after the beginning of the 20th century, the population is nearly 5 million people. As the Scottish traveller James Muirhead objectively calls it in his book of the same name, the land of contrasts is like a coin with two sides. One is that of a fast-growing city, a hub of industry and technical innovation. At the same time, the other is the challenges of resettlement, crime rates, poverty and a sense of suffocation. The American dream symbol – high-rise buildings, skyscrapers, large neighbourhoods are both a beautiful landscape seen from afar, and a gloomy image as the gaze approaches the details. The Danish-American innovator-photographer and journalist Jacob Rees gave an adequate and necessary sobering look in his book dated 1890. "How the other half lives."[8]Reese's photographs, which form the basis of the book, show the harsh reality of a vast group of New Yorkers living in ghettos and dormitories, which he calls the "other half."

On one side is the description of Muirhead, who writes,"... the connoisseur who hopes to see the Palazzo Pitti or the Dresden Gallery in every big city, the sociologist who will look for different customs and costumes on every corner... can refrain from a visit to this country. But on the other hand, the man who is interested in how civilisation works under

---

[8]Jacob August Rees, How the Other Half Lives.

completely new conditions, who can make concessions and adapt his perceptions, who appreciates the promising experiments in politics, sociology and education..., who is ready to evaluate the novelties for their usefulness, unless I am mistaken, will find compensation for the Swiss Alps, the Italian Lakes or the Gothic Cathedral... ". [9]And on the other side of the coin are Reese's photographs, which show a family of seven people and different generations living within a room, a dormitory, a ghetto.[10]

The transformation of the "boiling cauldron" into a homogeneous nation requires the creation of a common semiotic model that, when seen, evokes in mind a sense of Americanism to replace Europeanism. The foundations of any empire, whose metaphysical and even instinctive goal is to create a civilisational model, are laid by a sense of unity of models – from the most visible part –architecture, through literature, cultural customs and events, and finally reaching the kitchen. When it acquires a complete form, this order of civilisation can and should naturally be exported to the world, especially when there is a claim to exclusivity. This particular aspect acquires the dimensions of cultural hegemony, which is discussed in the following sections.

Umberto Eco rightly notes in his *"Treatise on General Semiotics"* that *"ideas are signs."*[11]The understanding and expression of the American ideal of a universal state is most visibly projected onto architecture. Certain details, shapes and symbols always

---

[9]James Muirhead, The Land of Contrasts, p. 8
[10]The photograph *" Room in a tenement),* ", 1910. , Jacob Rees.
[11]Umberto Eco, Treatise on General Semiotics, p. 197

carry specific mental associations. For example, the laurel wreath is always associated with absolute power and the imperial title. That is why Napoleon, at his coronation on December 2, 1804, is depicted by Jacques-Louis David with a laurel wreath with his hands holding the crown, all insignia of the supreme, poeticised and revered figure of the emperor. State symbols have also adopted certain animalistic forms, pointing to certain qualities characteristic of a people or nation towards what is intended as an intimation. In essence, this use has a semiotic meaning to be evoked in the mind when a particular symbol is seen. Whether it is the lion typical of the British Empire, depicted on the majestic marble and stone statues in front of state institutions, or in the specific American version – the use of the eagle as a symbol that should direct the mind to a specific connotation. The bald eagle was chosen as a state symbol in 1782 at the Second Continental Congress after three commissions failed to agree on the exact appearance of the coat of arms. In the end, Charles Thomson, the Secretary of Congress, combined the proposals of the three committees, which included a small image of an eagle, making it look majestic and enormous, occupying a central place in the idea that is still used today. Subsequently, the coat of arms stands as the cap of all official documents, banknotes and buildings. Even in the change of appearance of New York, in the construction of the Chrysler building, one of the symbols of the city and the state, metal heads of eagles were used to decorate the facade.

For about half a century, the significant influx of European settlers shaped the city's appearance similar to the great European capitals. There are many examples. The armoury of the 71st Regiment, located on 33rd Street and Park Avenue, is modelled on the Municipality of Siena, Italy. From the general plan to an almost exact copy of the tower. In the 1920s and 1930s, it was used as a boxing and music hall until it was demolished and a skyscraper was built in its place. It is the skyscraper that replaces most of the mansions that copy different European styles – from mansions in the style of the Second Empire in France, through German Gothic to the Napoleonic Empire. In 1899, a triumphal arch called Dewey was erected in honour of General George Dewey.

The photo materials show that it is very similar to the arch in Berlin, especially with the horse-drawn carriage on top of it. The arch was demolished only a year later, and the sculptures moved to Charleston. However, the first Triumphal Arch in New York, erected in 1871, still stands. Other examples of the city's iconic buildings are the Waldorf Astoria Hotel, which was demolished in 1928, and the Empire State Building was erected. It is the new style that replaces the European architecture and appearance of the city. This architectural style will take over much of the world later. It will be perceived as a symbol of success and economic prosperity – constructing skyscrapers of concrete, steel and glass. Although not all buildings reminiscent of Europe's past have been demolished and rebuilt, the appearance of all major cities in the United States is changing rapidly to such an extent that the skyscraper becomes their symbol, with a common lower cityscape along with a common urban lower panorama around them.

The book *"The Fountainhead"* by the American writer of Russian origin Ayn Rand through the main character – the architect Howard Roark raises in high-value individualism, the free market and mind, as well as the skyscraper, as a collective image of the listed virtues and as the supreme achievement of a new culture different from the European.

The desire for diversity is reflected in all spheres of life. Nevertheless, it is consciously understood by all or just a particular circle of researchers or elite. An obvious example is the manifestations in one of the forms of communication that unite people en masse – sports. For instance, in Europe, classic football is gaining momentum, invented as a professional game in England, but with a much more ancient character as a sport (Europe, China, ancient Greece, Japan, and even Central America in a much more brutal and cynical inhumane version). Rugby was played for the first time in the United States in 1861, and since 1876 the name American football has been officially accepted. Although the game is played by hand, the common name remains simply Football, while the European game of the same name is called "soccer". American football is also becoming the most popular sport in the young country, evolving at all ages. This game is not the only example of an attempt to escape the feeling of the Europeanism in the field of sports. Basketball was invented as a professional game in Springfield, Massachusetts, in 1891. Baseball as we know it today as a game was further developed in the United States from the English original. All these mass sports impose another characteristic feature, which is subsequently transmitted worldwide – the mass attendance of spectators, which takes place in large stadiums. The culture in the United States borrowed the name Arena from Ancient Rome, following the example of the great arena for gladiatorial battles – the Colosseum in Rome and all the other large amphitheatres in the empire.

The picture of American society would not be complete without mentioning the particularly important process of combating racial segregation against African Americans. Segregation takes extremely harsh forms, spreading to every area of American society – from using various toilets for whites and blacks in the 1920s and 1930s to restrictions on people of colour in sports clubs, restrictions on the education system, banks, etc. Only after the complete overcoming of the social division between whites and blacks can the form of the new nation be considered complete. However, at the end of the 20th and 21st centuries, there were still partial cases, significantly an increase in intolerance towards Spanish-speaking new migrants coming from Mexico and South America. That is, the nation's problem is not cured but simply blunted and then channelled into a new form. Particularly indicative is the complexity of tolerance, which distorts the art forms in the 21st century, with the presence of a quota principle accepted as an essential condition – men-women, white-black, etc. It is a problem and a process which will only escalate in time.

After the middle and end of the 19th century and at the very beginning of the 20th century, the United States grew into an economic giant. However, still, the external manifestation is more of a political dwarf on the international stage. It has changed since two points in time – the first was the Spanish-American War of 1898, and the second was the end of the First World War and the country's exit from the state of isolationism.

§ 2. The economic considerations of the political system

Historical facts and events by themselves as events mean nothing without being put in context, without being explained as part of a general process that in turn creates a model. For example, noting the fact that until 1840 in the United States, there was less than 4,500 km of the rail network, gives us nothing but a simple fact. Even if it is noted that by 1860, 20 years later, the railway network was already over 43,000 km, it did not provide clarity for a complete model but could be explained as a general economic boom. But if others are added to these two facts, for example:

- the completion of the first Transcontinental railway line, with a length of 3077 km, in 1869.

- the creation of the largest steel plant by Andrew Carnegie in Pittsburgh in the 80s of the 19th century, which supplied the railways with sleepers, and until 1900 is already the world's largest steel producer with 10,000,000 tonnes per year;

- In 1832, the painting professor Samuel Morse began experimenting with the possibilities of electricity, impressed by what he saw as an experience in Europe. In 1938 he successfully transmitted the first telegram by his newly patented recording telegraph.

If steel sleepers are the basis of rail transport, then the Morse telegraph has extraordinary communication influence. More interesting, however, is the synthesis that is created between the two. The telegraph connection helps for accurate train schedules to be created. Improving communication means solving all types of issues and processes faster – from the administrative ones to the business environment. The given examples from only two areas can be supplemented in dozens of others, but the final interpretation and conclusion will always be the same.

Based on the set of facts and processes considered in a given period of time, a general model can be made of what is happening in the young country. The processes that take centuries in Europe are tested, refined and applied here in a much shorter period of time. It leads to generating enormous energy, which shapes the new nation. Political development is directly related to the economic and social processes considered in their entirety. As a result, it creates the conditions for exporting the political model of which the developed economic system is a part.

The economic and political processes that take place shape the image of the new American society and its character. It lays the foundations of a different culture and civilisation, which is gradually moving away from the European one. Understanding the issue requires considering several interpretations of what culture and civilisation are. The contradictory definitions of Oswald Spengler, Fernand Braudel and Samuel Huntington are impressive.

In his outstanding work "The Decline of the West", Oswald Spengler presents civilisation as a consequence of culture once it has become history. *"Civilisation is the Inevitable Fate of Every Culture"*[12], he writes. Spengler does not view world history as assembled from chronologically successive epochs from Antiquity to Modernity. Rather as a synthesis of different cultures with their own germ, peak and then sunset, which turns them into civilisations. He makes a revolutionary categorisation that does

---

[12] Oswald Spengler, "The Sunset of the West: An Attempt at the Morphology of World History," p. 61.

not place Europe at the centre of the world, which is undoubtedly influenced as thought by the time he wrote his work – the time before and during the First World War. Given the book's time of writing, delineating a common mega culture – Western European, including the United States – may be chronologically wrong. Samuel Huntington determined the existence of 9 civilisations after 1990, placing the countries of Western Europe in the area of the great Western civilisation, while the countries East of Austria were set in the area of the Orthodox. From the present point of view, the proper adjustment should separate American culture from the common European one, more precisely as its branch, or even a new sprout that grows on its own. Spengler rightly notes that the processes of culture are inward, enriching and developing it, while the processes of civilisation are outward. Given the pace of economic development, American culture develops extremely dynamically, maturing prematurely, in a much shorter period of time, unlike the European one, taking some achievements "for granted". It makes it simpler for future consumer civilisation, which will take this model out into the world. If Spengler's model is used as a basis and further developed, American culture and civilisation are subsequently based on and exported through economic progress. In essence, the future consumer world is a synthesis between culture and economy, based on political decisions.

Undoubtedly, the most accurate and complete definition of "civilisation" comes from Fernand Braudel in *"A history of Civilisations"*. He defines the term extremely precisely as at least ambiguous. The etymology of the word can be traced from Italy through Dante to England, where the elite singular is used, which distinguishes the advanced world from the "other", in fact, the one that is misunderstood. Following Spengler's example, the plural appears after 1819, when different historical cultures, or periods, are distinguished. Braudel quoted French historian Charles Seignobos as jokingly was saying that *"civilisation is the roads, the ports and the wharfs."* A kind of way to show that civilisation is not just spirit or art. It is the basis of American civilisation – the synthesis between culture, economics and politics.

Conversely, in terms of the economy and the facts related to the country's economic life, it is worth noting the merit for developing mining and trade processes in the Western States and their social role. From 1840 until the very end of the 19th century, the first economic peak in the western part of the country was observed, which was expressed first in the Gold Rush in California, and later in Colorado and other states. There is even a curious process of initial explosion of activity, followed by almost complete extinction. One such example is the mining town of Creed in Colorado, wherein in 1890, large silver deposits were discovered. In the following years, between 150 and 300 new residents arrived in the town daily, seeking benefits despite the inconvenient location, located in a canyon and allowing the presence of only one straight street. Even this is a sign of ephemerality. When the price of silver started to fall sharply, Creed would be almost depopulated at the end of the century[13].

---

[13]See Alan Brinkley, History of the American People

It is also worth noting the emergence of a new industry, which in the coming years will be among the causes of many of the military conflicts, started or with the participation of the United States – the beginning of oil production and use. In 1859 the businessman Edwin Drake managed to extract oil for the first time on American soil land. Despite the historical records of much earlier knowledge and oil production centuries ago, its use is limited due to the lack of technological advances in other areas of life. In the late 19th and early 20th century, its extraction takes place at the right time to become an integral part of American and world consumption. The first refinery in Pennsylvania was established. In 1870 John Rockefeller succeeded in creating an association of prominent businessmen in the oil industry to lay the foundations of a vast empire that would control almost entirely the extraction, production and marketing of petroleum products in the United States in the future. It sets the beginning of corporations, which begin to organise their own research centre and attract staff, in parallel with the state. Afterwards, Henry Ford develops his internal combustion engine in the 1890s. In order to be able in 1914 to present the production line officially as a mode of production and this discovery to fundamentally change the notion of consumer market and consumption. By the end of the 19th century, 1% of corporations manage over 30% of all production in the country. It contributes to economic progress, but on the other hand, calls into question the whole idea of equality in the country. The concentration of substantial financial resources is a prerequisite for developing an equally huge projection of the political ambitions of the corporations. This process has further intensified as a dynamic, both in the Great War of 1918 and in the future.

The English historian Paul Johnson notes that by 1914, all public sectors are small, tending to grow very rapidly, with the range of actual government activity varying between only 5 and 10% of GDP.[14] By comparison, in Germany, which is building a large state apparatus for social security and services under Bismarck, this share is twice as high – 18%, and in the UK, which follows the German example, is 13% of GDP[15].

One event changes this direction of movement in the American economy drastically and forever. On April 2, 1917, US President Woodrow Wilson delivered a speech to Congress, urging it to declare war on Germany and enter the Great War. The address begins with the sinking of passenger and merchant ships by German submarines and the violation of human rights. The German submarine war began in response to the naval blockade imposed by the Entente. One line of the speech makes a strong impression, and its interpretation could serve as a cornerstone to justify all future military action of the United States. At the end of one of the paragraphs, Wilson says: *"The current German submarine war against the trade is a war against all mankind*[16]. Truly, it turns out that civilisation is the roads, ports and wharfs - and it could be supplemented, at the end of the 20th century to nowadays – the civilisation also is the energy resources. The American economy will be tied to a constant state of war forever in order to sustain

---

[14]Paul Johnson, "Modernity. The world from the 20s to the 90s ", p. 21.

[15] Ibidem

[16] "The present German submarine warfare against commerce is a warfare against mankind." - Woodrow Wilson, War Messages, 65th Cong., 1st Sess. Senate Doc. No. 5, Serial No. 7264, Washington, D.C., 1917

life and the feeling of stability inside. And any war will be justified by a struggle for human rights and democracy, and in fact, President Wilson notes very precisely: *"Put this nation in the war once, and they will forget that there was ever such a thing as tolerance. The spirit of ruthless brutality will enter every fibre of our national life."*[17]

The First World War resulted in the enormous expansion of the state, both horizontally and vertically, in terms of powers. And thus its tendency to control and oppress citizens. War forever undermines the sense of privacy. It is also a convenient time to deal with the dissenters. In 1917 The Espionage Act was passed, and in 1918 – Anti-state activity law. From now on, freedom of speech and ideas cannot be considered in the same way, by default. The speeches of the socialist Eugene Debs, which by their nature oppose the war, led to his arrest and subsequent sentencing to 10 years in prison and the abolition of the right to vote. Woodrow Wilson calls him a traitor. One of Debs' speeches, part of his defence in court, becomes extremely popular in the country. In it, he talks about workers' rights, the frustration of their rights, damaged by low wages and endless work, at the expense of giant corporations and industry[18]. Paul Johnson notes that personal freedom and private property tend to stick together or fall together. The First World War and its end turned the American economy into a war machine, which President Eisenhower, in one of his famous speeches, warns about the

---

[17] Foster Rhea Dulles, "The United States since 1865," p. 263. Quoted by Paul Johnson in "Modernity," p. 2

[18] Debs' Speech of Sedition -
https://en.wikisource.org/wiki/Debs%27_Speech_of_Sedition

military-industrial complex, a subject that will be considered in the chapters further. The concentration of capital and control of the system was protected in Charles Van Heath's book *"Concentration and Control"* even before the war. The advice was successfully applied both by President Theodore Roosevelt in his "new nationalism" and under Franklin Delano Roosevelt and his New Course.

The process of expansion of state power and its influence is determined not only by the internal preconditions associated with the war but also by the significant contribution of US relations with European countries during and after the Great War. If before the beginning of the war the United States owed the central European banks 3 billion, after the end, the countries of Western Europe owe the United States 14 billion.[19] The ratio to the current value of money shows that 1 billion dollars from 1918 would worth almost 19 billion today. It means a 14 billion debt from 1918 today would be 262 billion. And at the then-standard, they were paid in gold. After the end of the war, European countries found themselves in difficulties in paying off debts, creating a closed and vicious circle, which would subsequently lead to the outbreak of the next and greatest war in human history. France is trying to get its money from Germany, which cannot pay. After the payment of the first instalment of the military reparations, Germany falls into crisis. In 1923 France occupied the Ruhr area, which had the opposite effect on the

---

[19]See Hristina Mircheva, Contemporary History - The World in the History of the 20th Century, p. 111

country and its currency in the medium term. American banks lend to Germany, which in turn has to pay off the Entente countries. In essence, the happening of a new world war is predetermined to happen even in the peace treaties after the end of the Great War. It becomes clear that American aid is never just aid, but interest and return are always sought.

The enormous energy that Europe's gold accumulates, along with the corporations, turn the years after the war into the "Roaring Twenties" and, in fact, portend a real economic storm that would lead to the Great Depression. In the 1920s, they used to be called the crazy years in Europe and were associated not only with economic stabilisation but also with the rise of radical currents in politics. A life of credit calms France and Britain, creating a sense of normalcy. The Dawes Plan of August 1924 soothes the tensions created after the occupation of the Ruhr area, introduces relief for Germany's military reparations, and creates conditions for American concerns to enter European politics and economics. In the United States, in addition to the economic boom, gangsterism began to flourish due to the introduction of the Prohibition and the ban on the sale of alcohol (1920-1933). The turbulent years create the conditions for the development and imposition of the consumer type of society, which builds the culture to live on credit and the illusory feeling of a high standard. The illusion of the consumer is a profit for the financial capital and the corporations. As with any other time in history – this is a bubble that always bursts. Such consequences of an economic boom and then falling into the abyss always follow large-scale social and societal processes. After the First World War, we see the rise of the 1920s and the Great Depression. Then the Second World

War, followed by the calm and leisurely years of the 50s and 60s of the 20th century. The collapse of the Soviet system and the chance of the United States to build a unipolar world, a chance ultimately irretrievably worn out and used for selfish purposes in the following wars, until the bursting of the credit and property bubble in 2008 and the global economic crisis. The benefit of the enormous economic and financial capital is at the expense of the minor participant in the economic processes. The social inequality functions like the opening of scissors and begins as a visible process there in order to be able to reach the state it has at the moment, two decades since the beginning of the 21st century. The idea of individualism plays a bad joke, as it imposes a sense of influence on people. In fact, the real political and economic influence lies in the capabilities and ambitions of corporations, lobbyists, and the ruling elite. The economic dimensions of the political system would not be complete without paying attention to the general development of society. The power of the big capital is rooted in several areas: the infinitely inflated and branched state administration. In its infancy, the idea of a meritocratic system, devoid of the shortcomings of patrimonialism and clientelism, leads to effective administration and, hence, the general well-being of the state and the individual. Francis Fukuyama examines this administrative model in great detail in his works on political order and decay. Consumer life is a synthesis of the integrity of economics, politics, culture and education. In the specific American case (and later the general world), this means that the life on credit, the slow and gradual decline of the educational system towards the creation of a low-educated population, highly dependent on the information flows of radio, television, and subsequently, the Internet can be easily guided in the desired direction. Regardless of the feeling of a free spirit, free will, it turns out; decision-making is not in the hands of the sovereign. Even the form of elections as a legitimate way to elect representative power is questioned. One such example was 1960 Presidential elections when the Democrat John F. Kennedy was elected President. The victory is with a difference of 120,000 votes, out of a total of 69 million voters. In Paul Johnson's words, Kennedy's strength lies in his charm, youth, and popularity, but also in *"an efficient, ruthless political apparatus ran by his brother Robert."*[20]

A society of abundance[21] gives a sense of security and justice, but only when when one does not look in detail and depth, in time citizens freely and voluntarily, sometimes unconsciously, assign part of their rights to the state, which protects them from constant real or false threats from outside and inside. In other words – every strong state needs a figure of an enemy, internal or external, in order to justify its own powers. In the case with the US, the threat comes first from the Soviet Union until its collapse, and since the end of the 20th century, the threat comes from international terrorism. The peaceful years after the Second World War, bringing stability and a sense of serenity, create the conditions for bringing out the American idea of culture, modernity and, in general, an example of a proper way of living.

---

[20] Paul Johnson, Modern Times: A history from the Twenties to the Eighties, p. 499.

[21] John Galbraith, The Affluent society, Mariner Books. 1958

"Oxford History" of the 20th Century" gives an exact example of some of the different views of that time: *The bizarre fins of the cars symbolise the sparkle of brilliance at the time. Michael Harrington's The Other America (1962) talks about poverty that still exists amid abundance. More than 20% of the population continues to live in households below the government's "poverty line"*[22] The moment of cultural hegemony occurs – the time of fast life and fast food, jeans and chewing gum, the era of multi-million cinema, further developed since the 30s, as the most successful form of propaganda and creating the cultural model which conquers the world.

§ 3. Cultural hegemony – the great success

The view from a distance, which measures an interval of time over 100 years, comparable to a few generations, giving a long term projection, shows that a state which has hegemony over culture, social order, and education can be called a hegemon. The remarkable clash of models, which are inherently different in their views of the individual and the society, begins roughly after the First World War and around the 1930s. It lasts until the end of the Cold War. The three major models for society that confront each other directly are:

- The model of the American dream – the free individual, free activity, mass culture and the assumed, and even necessary, division of society into classes;

––––––––––––––––––––––––––

[22] Michael Howard, Oxford History of the 20th Century, p. 201

- The Soviet type of society – equality, brotherhood, a victory of the working class. An attractive and magnetic model of culture that manages to ignite people from both Europe and the world with its ideas;

- The racial model of Nazi Germany – the idea of racial superiority, but built around a single race and defining all others as weaker or even superfluous. It is an attempt to create the perfect society and the perfect person. A morally wrong, blood-soaked model that ends on a massive scale with the end of World War II. The fact is that even today, there are groups that develop this idea in a neo-Nazi version, both in Europe and elsewhere in the world. And in some cases, even admitted and encouraged by the official governments or with its participation in them.

Opposing one model to another always leads to positive consequences, expressed through innovations – at a technological, social and cultural level. One of the most accurate examples of the opposition of different cultural models in the interwar period can be cited in the Soviet Union and its film industry. The Soviet director, and one of the pioneers in the art of film making, Sergey Eisenstein, created a revolution in celebration of the Revolution. In his movie "The Battleship "Potemkin" from 1925, he is doing something that has never been done before. In one of the last scenes, attention is drawn to the waving red flag, a reference to the Soviet flag, albeit with a different official meaning in the symbolism used in the navy. When making the film, the cinema is still in black and white and here comes the surprise – the viewer sees the scarlet flag in colour. Eisenstein processes the tape frame by frame, painting the flag by hand in each of a total of 108 frames to show the superior model that stands out from the rest. The symbol, bringing a revolution in the cinema, the forerunner of the future multibillion-dollar industry in the West, comes to show the superiority of the Soviet cultural and social, and why not technological, model over all others. Eisenstein's techniques, which became a model, would later be applied in Hollywood and studied by actors and directors. In essence, innovations in cinema that help the American cultural model emerge gradually as a hegemon after World War II originate in the Soviet Union and are part of the intercultural opposition. Eisenstein is one example, some others are Lev Kuleshov and the theatrical figure Konstantin Stanislavsky, whose theories and models are still studied today in the film academies in the United States. The biggest names in the film art pay homage in their films to the scene with the pogrom on the steps in Odessa by the "Battleship "Potemkin". Francis Ford Coppola in "The Godfather" twice recreates the feeling – first in the first part of the film of 1972, and then in the third one of 1990. Also, in the third part of "Star Wars" from 2005, George Lucas recreates Eisenstein's scene using the same technique. After all, even when models are opposed, borrowing and continuity can be observed but more importantly - respected. However, valuable achievements remain, and their significance and origin should not be overlooked or forgotten.

After the First World War, the centre of science and culture is still located in Europe. Human capital, built over centuries and withstood various persecutions over time (from the persecution of Jews in different parts of Europe between the 15th and 19th centuries to more local religious persecutions in France in the 17th century), is tempted cross the Atlantic starting a new life in the politically attractive young country. It is slowly and gradually happening that European scientists of different nationalities and religions build America's scientific capital. An interesting example from the beginning of the 20th century, connected with the automobile industry, which is one of the factors for the complete change of the American society, is the construction of the most famous for its time Model T of the company Ford. The model is the main work of the Hungarian scientist Josef Galamb, who receives an exceptional education first in his homeland and later in Germany. In the German company Adler, he acquires the best practical knowledge. He participates in a process in which each car engine must be assembled entirely by one person. Two years later, he becomes a part of Ford's employees, who, until the invention of the Model T, has assembled their cars with mostly pre-purchased parts.

Gradually, the example of Galamb goes beyond the particular case and becomes a trend. In addition to the free choice of going to the US, the enormous waves of scientists who immigrate to the States are associated mainly with an immediate threat to their lives and work. In the 1930s, more than 1,000 Jews, or those of Jewish descent, successfully leave Germany and Eastern Europe for fear of persecution. The sensitivity of the brain drain for the period can be illustrated with simple statistics – within ten years from 1930 to 1940, 12 Nobel laureates left Europe and Germany for going to the United States. Seven of these scientists are Jews – Albert Einstein, Nils Bohr, Otto Levy, and others. Other names include scientists such as Enrico Fermi, the creator of the first nuclear reactor, Wolfgang Pauli, one of the pioneers of quantum physics, nominated by Einstein for the Nobel Prize.

The most significant ideological clash in the world begins with the end of the Second World War. US politicians, despite the war against Nazism, turn a blind eye to the ideas and origins of scientists, as long as there is an immediate benefit to the rapidly growing military-industrial complex. The Machiavellian practice led to the creation of the secret Operation "Paperclip". More than 1,600 German scientists, some of them Nazis with a background, began to work in the United States. Some of them are called the "von Braun Group", named after Werner von Braun, who is among the elite of German rocket engineers. He himself adapts successfully to the American society, despite the proven Nazi bias – he is a member of the NSDAP although he provides amended information about the year of his membership, but he is also an SS officer with the rank of Unterschurmführer (Lieutenant). During his years in the United States, the media repeatedly raised the issue of this part of his personal history and his work on V-2 missiles. Von Braun's team is at the heart of the American rocket program and the creation of Saturn rockets for sending people into space.

Operation "Paperclip", as a part of the whole process of brain draining to the United States, predisposed to a favourable state policy, is the basis for creating scientific elite in the country and, for a large extent tracing the ascending order path in the field of science. The moral cost is in the use of capacity not only for science but also for the needs of the military-industrial complex.

Yet, until the first years after WWII, the world's intellectual and cultural elite is still located in Europe. Cambridge historian Tony Judt says that America, and New York in particular, still seem provincial in terms of intellectual life. Nothing comes from America that can be compared to the European scene. And Paris is once again, and for the last time, capital of the world.[23] After these last years of cultural hegemony, the change brought about by the whole generation of European intellectuals who have moved to the United States could be felt. The idea of the power of the individual begins to conquer the world and compete with the concept of the collective power of the East. Our mind is so structured that it seeks what is hidden, wants what is forbidden, and desires to taste what society forbids. This is what happens with the societies in the Soviet sphere of influence. Even if the competitive system is not better, it looks better because it is inaccessible in its mass. Idealisation is the force that gives the necessary impetus to the consumer culture. The poeticised dream of the free spirit, of the freedom of differences, leads to the hegemony of the consumer society at the end of the 20th and the beginning of the 21st century. At the heart of this understanding is the postulate *"I am"* and hence its suffixes. *"I am different"* – in a society where everyone wears jeans and sneakers, in the end, it leads to sameness in difference. The illusory difference that feeds one's sense of significance is the invocation of the consumer instinct – the desire to own the latest car model, to wear a new collection of clothes, the snobbish feeling of the housewife – who wants the highest class and brand of a refrigerator because they see it as a projection of oneself in the dimension of the kitchen and appliances. Another sustainable statement in the emerging consumer culture is *"I am free"*. It turned out that, especially after America's baseless and unnecessary wars from the beginning of

---

[23]Tony Judt, Timothy Snyder, Thinking the Twentieth Century

the 21st century against terrorism, that the American citizen is ready to give up a number of his constitutional rights with the only promise of physical safety. It is based on the threat posed by the state to the physical existence of citizens, because in essence, by starting a war based on lies, the state itself undermines the security of its citizens, reaching a vicious circle from which the latter suffer. *"I am free"* turns out to be a blank expression that has been repeated for too long as a mantra has taken a special place in the American consciousness, part of the idea of the American dream. Fukuyama describes how dozens of security agencies have overlapping functions, each trying to control the other and all together trying to monitor and control the citizens. The created fear of every possible external enemy (in the period from the 50s to the beginning of the new 21st century, the "enemy" changes its shape, face, and name) makes the American entirely dependent and deceived. From this point of view, there is a huge difference in the minds of American citizens and Europeans. The lack of a real war with a real external enemy on its own continental territory deprives American society of what is happening in Europe and Britain – to realise the horror of military action and the ultimate conclusion of the physical war – the catastrophe. On this basis, there is no commitment of the state in the social sphere to create a real welfare state, as we have as developed in Europe after the Second World War. What the United States creates as a model is non-committal, does not require a depth of vision and attention, but is basically "fast." The generally accepted stereotypes about the Europeans still turn out to be true – in Italy and France, the pleasure of appreciating good food, the process of drinking coffee is valued, as it is even in Turkey or in general – joie de vivre. Eastern Europe and Russia also have a similar type of hedonism, the "joy of life," because its value is appreciated. All the fast-food chains that eventually conquered the world originated from the United States – speed, at the expense of pleasure. And from there – the quality, at the expense of pleasure.

An obvious difference, for which a special type of effort has been made in recent years to blur and distort, is even in the idea of creating and building a home. Over the centuries, the European model of monolithic construction has been developed. From Bulgaria, where the concept of eternity is recreated through the stone inscriptions of the Khans of the First Bulgarian State, to Italy, where Roman construction is still given as an example of eternity, and throughout Europe – independence is equivalent to a monolithic house – built of stone, brick, later concrete. A completely different type of construction is being developed in the United States – light, prefabricated, and mostly from timber. One of the possible explanations is due to the climatic features and natural phenomena, but there are still family buildings from the early 20th century, which are built of stone. The model of rapid construction is combined with a life on credit but also a life on rent. The most dangerous trend that has taken over Europe is the feeling of security from living on rent. Such security is not security. It is a rule, confirmed during every economic and financial crisis, as well as during and after every property and mortgage bubble. In the end, the one who suffers the most is the poor man, the one who is completely dependent on the market's will. This is the power of the financial capital – when society is controlled by loans, mortgages, rents – the security is in the hands of the landlord, lender, etc., but not in the hands of the citizen. The whole model of money, banks and consumption is based on the idea of the power of the big corporation, the big owner and the big capital. And big the capital does not need citizens who own their land or property. This vicious and perhaps still temporary model during the years of bipolar opposition, and then in the short time of the American unipolar experiment, receives tremendous support through the methods of cinema and music. Besides manipulating public opinion during crises and mass events, art forms are first charged with the responsibility of spreading the American Dream worldwide.

In the years after the end of the Cold War, in the countries of Eastern Europe, where previously students studied Russian as a second compulsory language, a gradual replacement with English began. It is the best investment to control a whole generation – through language, it will understand both cinema and music, but it will also broadly seek and find information. The soft power used through language and its widespread distribution ensures that a large proportion of young people who grow up with English from a very early age, in addition to their own, will gravitate around the informational and cultural influence of the American model. Language and culture are like seeds sown in fertile soil that will grow in unconscious dependence. First, through the influence of cinema – the perception of Anglo-Saxon names as a norm, although not in the nominal tradition, but certainly in everyday life, and even in the naming of pets, with all the conventionality of everyday life, is something very typical of the East-European countries. Subsequently, the opening of the labour market through student visas for this same generation, raised in absentia with the American dream. All that remains is to show these young people the showcase of the American life - the greatness of New

York or Washington. This is until one reaches Alaska or one of the central states and confronts the reality of American society, beyond the coast – extreme disinterest in the history, geography and peculiarities of the world outside the country, poor education, simplified cities and towns. It turns out that the United States, after all, is a showcase represented by the cities-symbols, as already mentioned – the country of contrasts. The condition for success is to be approved by the one who directs and determines the influence. How "modern" or "successful" a country or society is, is determined by the bearer of the model. Usually, the process is completed when the population is placed in absolute dependence – financial, economic, military and informational. Then the formal acceptance comes with entering this "elite" club of established democracies – a hypocritical and false form of freedom in which the shackles are spiritual as well as physical.

The great success of the American cultural model is expressed in the right instinct for understanding human nature – the one that, when is tempted, breaks. The human nature which is always looking for the fast way – to success, knowledge, and everything else. Why to read a book in its entirety if you can read an edited and abridged version? In its mass, public instinct is thirsty for quick knowledge, quick lessons, and quick ostentation. For example, why is it necessary to spend many hours, days, and even months reading a classic like "The Count of Monte Cristo" if we want to learn about suffering and the bitter experience of success, providence, and the desire for unconditional help, because of the ultimate belief that being Good is a choice and nature? Isn't it easier to read the biography of a person, presented through a series of quotes about good and evil in a fashion magazine, and nowadays – on the Internet? Short "infographics" speak of the bitter experience, replacing the length and depth of the text with symbols. The decline of the mass person sends him back to the cave way of communication – through symbols, through "emoticons". The beauty of thought is replaced by quick knowledge and quick results. The American dream touches that part of the human soul which has highest desire for speed in everything – results, knowledge, or even the speed to forget a wrongdoing. The great film, again a Hollywood production, "Devil's Advocate", starring by Al Pacino, very accurately expresses the ease with which one can stumble into the temptation of a sense of success, of power, of growth. Al Pacino's character – the Devil himself – says that this is the goof of all time – *"look, but don't touch; touch but don't taste; taste, but don't swallow"*, and yet you always go to extremes. It is the advantage of the American dream as a model, which of course, has its many exceptions – it is easily assimilated, does not require depth and promises success. And that is the reason why it conquers Europe and partly Asia after the end of the Cold War. That is also the period in which the idea of the American order – a world regulated by a single superpower left as a sole hegemon – has been tested. It does not take long for the test to begin to be confirmed and reaffirmed as unsuccessful. Still, societies are prone to profanation, especially given the remoteness of the last great war, more than 70 years ago. The forgotten horror of war makes people live lightly, enjoying easy times, despite being full of local conflicts, but slowly pushing the system to the moment of collision or catastrophe, which will make times difficult again and require both depth of vision, knowledge, and the skills and efforts to survive.

2

Transition and Crisis of the American Exceptionalism

§ 1. The end of the "soft power" idea

"Because friendship won with money, not with the greatness and nobility of the spirit, is bought, but does not exist; and when you need it, you can't count on it. In general, people are less likely to offend the one who arouses their love than the one they fear. Because love is based on a relationship, on gratitude, and because people are bad, they can always break it when they find it profitable. And the fear is due to the threat of punishment, which never leaves the person."[24]

In the 19th century, a metaphor for the meaning and application of power gained popularity: a carrot attached to a stick by a donkey rider tricks the donkey into continuing to walk in the direction chosen by the rider, despite his stubbornness, chasing the constantly receding carrot. In essence, this metaphor has a dual meaning. On the one hand, the illusion of reward (carrot) manifested as a tool through the stick without realising the manipulation. The comparison of a human or a state subject with the donkey is inherently cynical, as it equates the intellect of the animal with the issue being compared. To conceal real intentions, methods of manipulation at the level of states and societies are

---

[24]Niccolo Machiavelli, The Prince

widespread. They are like a beautiful package, seducing the taste and imagination, hiding the rotten product inside. When the United States promotes freedom, free trade sounds like a glimpse into the bright future, and it actually means satisfying the appetite of the American economy and corporations. At the end of the Cold War, Gorbachev was promised that NATO would not expand to the east. However, in the realm of real politics, there is a distance between a promise and a contract called a lie. And no one judges the winner, or at least not in the short term. The promise was not fulfilled, and the result is observed to this day – all NATO enlargements over the years, which ultimately form, first – the Balkan Corridor, second and greater – an attempt to encircle Russia and as far away from the European Union. The real goals are hidden by creating a shiny packaging, changing its shape and appearance as needed. Manifestations of manipulation can be directed inward to the society of a country. Gradually, after the attacks of September 11, 2001, the propaganda machine of the power creates a feeling of fear in societies, which is voluntarily ready to give up a number of its privileges of freedom in exchange for providing physical security. The threat of external enemies and international terrorism leads to the expansion of the apparatus of security agencies, which gain enormous power over the control and surveillance of society. In this way, the citizen enters in an unequal deal of privacy against "protection against terrorism". Any attempt at enlightenment receives fierce persecution, for example – in the cases of Edward Snowden and Julian Assange. In the end, John Locke's *"Second Treatise on Governance"* confirms that the power of the rulers is only possible with the consent of the ruled ones. That is why it is vital for the government not to violate the integrity of the packaging; otherwise, the institutional decline will be seen very quickly, both at the level of morality and efficiency. When elite of a state is willing to treat its own society the way the rider treats the donkey, means two things:

First, on an internal level – nothing good is ahead for the state and society. In the best case – a feeling that there is a mistake in the system on the part of society and its cleansing – in a peaceful/electoral way, or through revolution; and in the bad – if society has finally lost its old reflexes of correctness, morality and thirst for progress – the decline of the whole state, including the possibility of its fragmentation. It is an opportunity that is discussed ahead in the chapters.

Second – on the external level – if the elite's attitude towards their own is like that of the rider to the donkey, it means that the external manifestation of Machiavellianism will be many times greater. Unilateral goals and ambitions lead to methods and measures that would lead to success in the short run, but in the long run lead to a blurring of the objective view of the world, a sense of irreplaceability and at the same time proving to the world that substitutability is not simply possible, but a methodically constructed reality.

Here also appears the second aspect of the metaphor of the carrot and the stick, the manifestation of which is much clearer and better understood after falling off the aura of exceptionalism. The second aspect does not include a donkey being deceived by a free-standing carrot in front of his eyes. It is much more direct, yet with the possibility of being cynically presented as "freedom of choice." The subject has the opportunity to choose a carrot – as the offered "benefit", as the fulfilment of a wish, or the bludgeon – if he does not make the "right" choice. The false sense of choice is among the undesirable, which becomes desirable under the threat of sanction. It is the model adopted by Washington, except concerning all its allies and all other countries. If the unilateral will is not fulfilled – the use of the sanctions tool follows – the stick of the considered metaphor.

The use of this method goes beyond the accepted understanding of "soft power". It results from the already removed mask of benevolence, which does not preclude the repetition of established patterns of freedom, Atlantic solidarity and protection against terrorism. At its core, the true soft power of the United States lies in the cultural model already discussed and its dissemination. After the end of the Second World War, the nation, created and established in the 19th and the first half of the 20th century, began to spread its influence in Europe, destroyed by the horrors of war. The Marshall Rescue Plan, adopted in 1948, played a significant role in the success of the long-term goal and covering almost all Western European countries. For the period from April 3, 1948, until June 30, 1953, beneficiary countries receive more than 14 billion dollars in the form of direct aid and loans.[25] In its current exchange rate, the amount is over 150 billion. The Marshall Plan is not the only US initiative in the direction to bind Europe. Stanford economist Daphne Raymond notes in "The Marshall Plan today" a number of other programs that are close in monetary value or equal to those invested through the Marshall Plan. For example,

---

[25]John Agnew, J. Nicholas Entrikin, The Marshall plan today - model and metaphor, Routlege, 2004, p. 110

the Mutual Defense Assistance Program (MDAP) alone has been allocated 11 billion for defence and armament. *"If we look at this broader framework of aid, Raymond writes, "which still gives us only a partial picture; we understand that during the seven post-war years, Western Europe has been given $ 29.3 billion in aid."*[26] Separately, the countries are directly bound to the United States, outside the mentioned general programs.

The United Kingdom, for example, receives additional direct loans by the US amounting to more than $ 4.5 billion at the then exchange rate outside the Marshall Plan. It turns out that the cultural clash between the United States and the Soviet Union would not have the same direction and development without this long-term financial and military commitment presented as aid.

The battles in the name of the cultural model are fought by façade cultural organizations and individuals based on the CIA and other security agencies. Tony Judt calls these CIA operations and initiatives a "Marshall Propaganda plan."[27] Soft power is actually a well-disguised Machiavellianism. The whole idea of cultural superiority is based on the false pretence of a choice between the carrot and the stick. If the culture is the carrot, then the money and the loans are the stick — a noose from which there is no clear exit. The instincts of the European are dulled and honed by the feeling of a peaceful life after the 50s. With the possibility of a wider audience, every form of mass art is used for propaganda purposes. Creating a showcase model ensures that people of one

---

[26]Ibidim
[27]Tony Judd, Timothy Snyder, Thinking in the Twentieth Century, 271

or more generations will grow up with the idea of Americanism – they will dress according to a particular model, speak the language of a specific model, watch the movies of the model and build, in most cases unconsciously, their life again within the general American model. Furthermore, it is necessary to mark the film industry as a method of reaching the largest audience. When a country does not have its own mythology, due to its historical youth, mythology is created through cinema and borrowing from another's history. Thus, popular films based on American superheroes show just that – there is always an impending apocalypse in the plot (whether it is a natural disaster, an external enemy or aliens), and always in the centre there is standing a showcase city like New York, Washington or Chicago. The ultimate idea always shows the sacrifice of the American people for the common good of the world, and the viewer is always left with the view of an American-centric world. During the Cold War, the popular character John Rambo was created, which should blur the notion of the American failure in Vietnam with the idea of an all-powerful warrior-individualist. After the end of the Cold War, the image of the enemy was replaced by a stereotypical model of the cultivated negative character – either having a Slavic name or, by nature, callous, lying and prone to bigotry and constantly threatening the whole free society.

Soft power as a form of spreading influence does not work unilaterally to create and maintain the good image of a country. There is also a reverse direction, as already mentioned – the creation of a figure of the enemy to serve as an anti-example. The state of fear is nurtured in the minds of society in order to have the right motivation to fight against the "other". The whole ideological system of this type of society is built around two pillars – the one of consumption and life on credit and the other – of the fear of threat – terrorism, use of nuclear weapons, invasion of foreign armies, etc. In short– fear, spectacle and consumption.

The beginning of the 21st century revived and further developed the use of art for propaganda purposes. The expressiveness of art is used to suggest specific archetypes and aims to complete the image of the created enemy. The Cold War did not end the image of the "evil empire," as President Reagan called the Soviet system in his speech in 1983. On the contrary, it undergoes a transformation so that the negative image of Russia can be sustained in the 21st century. Ayn Rand, in "The Fountainhead", through the ideas of one of his negative characters, gives an extremely timeless example of the basis of power – you do not need swords or whips to rule over a man if you control his soul, you can rule over all mankind.[28]There is a sense of continuity between "then Russia" and "present Russia", both of which cannot be trusted(Similar connotations concerning "trust" can be found in the recent public discourse regarding China). This technique is also the "wedge" that is created and driven into the soul of society. In the absence of trust, given the conditions for

---

[28]If you manage to control the soul of one person, you will be able to rule over all humanity. The soul is important, Peter, the soul. Power is not exercised with whips, swords, fire or rifles. That is why rulers like Caesar, Attila or Napoleon have not achieved much. But this does not apply to us. What power is powerless is the soul, Peter. It must be broken. Insert a wedge into it, insert your fingers into the slot and then the person will be yours. You will not need a whip - he will bring it to you and ask you to whip it. Turn its essence upside down and its own mechanism will do the job for you. Use it against himself. ", Ayn Rand, The Fountainhead

"innate" suspicion of the "Other", in particular – Russia, there is no need for whips and swords to guide human behaviour. And this is the game in the long run – when there is no longer a generation that carries the critical impulse to doubt, there are still generations that determine their position based on art and not science. And although the truth is in the great library of European memory, it needs readers to search for it. Umberto Eco describes in great detail the process of creating an enemy.[29] The enemy has a specific set of characteristics. He has lost public trust and expectations; he is harmful because he threatens the collective (in this case – a "modern and free society"). Eco writes that war is an inevitability and a necessity in order to maintain order in society, to have active forces and a reason to remain united due to the presence of an enemy. The war is currently in the field of mind and for the mind. Who controls memory will control the future.

In the end, when the various beautiful packages are removed, the accurate content of the idea is revealed – the United States securing a huge European buffer, which is also a huge market for goods and loans. And in the long run – the elimination of the Soviet threat and the expansion of the sphere of influence throughout the world. The idea of American exceptionalism culminates with the end of the Cold War. There is only one superpower in the world that has the full power to determine all the parameters of being politically correct – from moral to material. After the end of the Cold War, for any state leader in the world, the meeting with the American president is equivalent to

---

[29]Umberto Eco, Creating the Enemy and Other Writings on Random Occasions.

the meeting with the emperor of the Roman Empire in its apogee. It is the only historic chance for the United States to show that it really is what it claims to be as an elite, that the world will indeed become a better place under the arbitration and tutelage of a single state. The bipolar world had one major advantage – it had a sense of order. Everyone knows where the other stands, and despite the Iron Curtain, the contact does not stop at the level of special services. It turns out that the world is a much safer place when the intentions are clear, and the demands for better order are in the field of competition and rhetoric. After the collapse of the bipolar system and the collapse of the Soviet Union, the difficult task of putting justice rhetoric into practice comes. Attempting to introduce a new order initially seems like a long-awaited dream that is one move away and can be caught. Fukuyama formulates his idea of the *"end of history"*, and the inevitability of liberal democracy defended and promoted by the United States. In the following years, the idea of the good hero begins to crack. Washington's actions are in stark contrast to the ideals of peace and freedom. Forced change of order because one state and its elite find it wrong does not mean freedom. The power hegemony, deprived of an understanding of the historical and cultural sense of order in the other players, turns out to be a desire for economic conquest, carried out through the methods of both force diplomacy and military aggression. Financial interests, together with the notion of exceptionalism, are gradually erasing the only ground for greatness – the culture of diversity and the inherited and then elevated position of one language as a universal tongue throughout the whole world. Even it is corrupted by the building of economic slavery and predatory appetite, as well as by the barbaric instinct to destroy what you do not understand.

It is appropriate to consider the Indian matter because the model of doing things is the same. The motives are the same. Just as the new nation is "dealing" with the Indian matter, so is it dealing with all the other countries and states in the world that have experienced the privilege of being "liberated." Each empire pursues its interests, but the difference is in the presence or absence of a creative instinct. The empire, which has the pretence and shows the properties of universality, leaves behind a culture and does not turn the countries that influence into chaos and ruins.

Joseph Nye, who is credited with using the term "soft power," sees economics as hard power. The last two decades, and more, have shown that the economy and its instruments are also part of the "soft power". Facade organizations, non-governmental organizations that operate throughout Eastern Europe and formally work for a non-profit purpose, are, in fact, becoming a conduit for the interests of a single state. The interference of outside-funded NGOs in the countries' education and judiciary systems is a real example of soft power. The weakness of countries, due to economic and military dependence, facilitates the penetration of structures that are allowed to shape public policy in areas of strategic importance. The rupture of America's "soft power" begins at the domestic level with the ability to see and acknowledge dependence. According to the traditional understanding of the term, soft power means the ability of a country to influence other countries in such a favourable way, through its good example or common values, that a common goal set by the state emitting soft power to be pursued. In fact, talking about common values begins to diverge abruptly from action in this direction. Satisfying the interests of the military-industrial complex and corporate giants and the idea of political infallibility thwarted the attempt to build an image of a defender of freedom and justice by showing the bully's face, the bad student who creates conflicts. The examples over time are not only concrete but also outline a clear trend that has the opportunity to manifest itself in real action in the near future.

An accurate example is the failure to organize a common coalition for the causeless invasion of Iraq and the start of the war in 2003. Subsequently, Edward Snowden announced in 2013 that the National Security Agency had eavesdropped on 35 world leaders for years, including those of EU countries.[30] The scandal caused is enormous, followed by calls from German Chancellor Angela Merkel, French President Francois Hollande, Dilma Rousseff from Brazil and others. Washington has officially confirmed that it does not eavesdrop and will not eavesdrop in the future, but no answer has been given for the past. Anti-Americanism is confirmed by several EU opinion polls between 2007 and 2013[31], showing a trend that a significant proportion of EU citizens are more receptive to the idea of pan-European security to replace the existing architecture under the umbrella of NATO. The topic of common European security has actively entered public rhetoric, but in practice, Europe is profoundly

---

[30]Anger Growing Among Allies on U.S. Spying - New York Times, 23.10.2013, https://www.nytimes.com/2013/10/24/world/europe/united-states-disputes-reports-of-wiretapping-in-Europe.html
[31]lMontiDatta, The Decline of America's Soft Power in the United Nations, International Studies Perspectives • August 2009, p. 3

dependent to afford a truly free will of action. French President Emmanuel Macron revived in 2018-2019 actively the talks in this direction, also including Russia in the general model of security. At the same time, Macron has faced the protests of the "Yellow Vests", and a free parallel can be drawn with other mass initiatives, working on a particular pattern over the years throughout Europe. For example, the Orange Revolution, the protests of 2013 in Ukraine and the ensuing coup, the protests in Georgia in 2019 and others. There are too few coincidences in history. The issue of security opportunities for the EU deserves more attention in the text ahead. Trust is like a porcelain cup that can never be the same again once broken, even glued. The cracks remain. The reasons for this process are rooted mainly within a country. When the internal content does not correspond to the external form, it always means that a crisis is coming – a crisis of the spirit, a crisis of self-acceptance, and ultimately – the bigger the state, the bigger the crisis it will cause in the world. The United States has the finished external form of a universal empire, but the content inside is, perhaps, forever doomed not to be completed in the desired pattern. One of the reasons for such a conclusion is the lack of historical experience and the historical youth of the country. Early maturation and early awareness of power entail the risk of missed knowledge. It is the main precondition for this huge country, at the moment when it is left alone on the global stage as a hegemon, not to know what to do with all the responsibility that arises from that victory. Yes, the United States won the Cold War, but it turned out to be a Pyrrhic victory because of the missed opportunity. The lack of a creative instinct, which not all states and nations carry as a talent, but the lack of historical time to develop one, leads to a primary, hedonistic and arrogant attitude towards the role as hegemon. At the expense of the rest of the world, the wild satisfaction of one's own needs leads to a 30-year period of military and economic barbarism.

§ 2. The economic and military barbarism of the United States

In 2020 the United States celebrated 244 years since it was established as a state. Statistics show that during 225 out of a total of 244 years of existence, the state is in a practical state of war or involved in an armed conflict against someone (including the War of Independence and any internal or border conflicts). For the entire period of its existence, the state has been at peace for only 19 years and viewed from another angle – a total of about 120 wars or conflicts involving or led by Washington for the short period of existence of two and a half centuries. The interpretation of these data, without exaggeration, means that the United States is one of the most militarized nations, unable to exist as a state without being in a state of war. It is reminiscent of President Wilson's words when the United States joined World War I – yet war is in every fibre of national life. The strong state is the result of the war, but even then, the strong state creates the war to maintain its power. The state of war, on the one hand, requires the presence of professionals to lead it, both at the diplomatic and field level, but also a state administration capable of solving problems. It is also the basis for the creation of a bureaucratic working machine before its subsequent suppression. Namely, dealing with clientelism and creating a meritocratic administration. On the other hand, a state of war creates a true community and unites the nation. It creates the idea of collective justice, and subsequently, this collective justice develops the ambition to regulate the world in its image. Preached individualism at the domestic level has been replaced at the national and supranational levels. The collective feeling and imposition of justice and retribution are much stronger than individual enmity and vendetta.[32]

However, the militarization of one country does not mean that the same country wins victorious wars. It is especially true of the United States because the wars it waged — including those the government doesn't like to talk about much — have a bilateral impact on external authority and society inside. Due to military spending and financing of operations (both secret and public), government indebtedness is barbaric towards one's own people. Both in the 1950s and at the beginning of the 21st century, the supply of the military-industrial complex led to a restriction of social policy. As Tony Judt mentions in 'Thinking the Twentieth Century", it's because war is not seen as a catastrophe. We go back again to the topic of historical experience. Washington's adventurism has always been paid expensively, first by its own society and then by the whole world. Within 20 years, the US economy has fallen into recession five times as a result of military conflicts, economic factors, and one of them is influenced by the so-called. "Asian flu". First, after the Korean War (1950-1953), the economy fell into a post-war recession, costing 56 billion dollars. It was followed by two recessions in 1957 and 1958, the so-called "The Eisenhower Recession", which acquires worldwide character, spreading from the United States to Canada and Europe. The next two recessions for the selected period dated 1960 and 1969-70. The

---

[32]Paul Johnson, Modern Times. The world from the twenties to the eighties.

same pattern of recession manifested itself in 1990 after the Gulf War. Therefore, the term "barbarism" is not used in the traditional sense of "different from the conventional notion of civilization", but as the behaviour of a warlike, greedy elite, which overshadows all the positive opportunities for the development of their own society and at its own expense. Inward-looking economic barbarism leads to a state that is the opposite of the welfare state in Western Europe. And in the long run, it will lead to the years of the decline of the United States.

Barbarism, directed outwards, begins with the Spanish-American War and the subsequent occupations of Nicaragua (1898-1899), Panama (1901-1914) and many others, part of a total of more than 120 US military participations. The use of nuclear weapons over Japan on August 6 and 9, 1945, is also barbaric. More than 200,000 are directly killed, most of them civilians, and it causes damages beyond any notion of civilization. Even the very intention of desired dropping a total of seven more bombs (one on August 19 and three in September and October 1945) means that the desire is not just to defeat the enemy, who has already been defeated, but to bring fear, with the cost of hundreds of thousands of innocents. At the end of the Cold War, a book entitled *"Other Losses"* by Canadian historian James Bacque was published. The official authorities are charged with refuting the data in the book, but there are also a sufficient number of historians who confirm its authenticity. In the first years after World War II, the US Army set up 19 camps in West Germany to temporarily detain surrendered German soldiers. The status of surrendered soldiers is changed to disarmed enemy forces to avoid the application of the Geneva Convention. More than 700,000 German prisoners of war were deliberately killed by starvation and cold. It turns out that the cultural and social model defended and imposed by the United States is not the bright dream of a free man, but a screen behind which are the same human traits that propaganda exposes as evil in the so-called totalitarian and authoritarian models.

After World War II, the United States pursued an aggressive policy of changing legitimate governments with installed puppet regimes and governments. Between 1947 and 1989, the government in Washington organized 72 attempts to replace the power in other countries[33], most often those from the Third World, but not only. The investigation of all these cases, and of secret operations in general, is a complicated process, as official information about them can always be rejected by the authorities, and if it is not, it may not be complete, even "cut". The US special services have succeeded in their efforts to overthrow governments and establish new, acceptable ones a total of 26 times. But this total number does not include all other CIA operations in organizing riots, suppressing them, assassinations attempts on leaders, and so on. It is important to follow not all of Washington's interventions but to mark those that outline and prove the existence of a common model in the formation of foreign policy and its definition as a barbaric act. Although in the context of the Cold War and the clash with the Soviet Union, the commemoration is important for rationalizing the hypocritical

---

[33]The U.S. tried to change other countries' governments 72 times during the Cold War, https://www.washingtonpost.com/news/monkey-cage/wp/2016/12/23/the-cia-says-russia-hacked-the- us-election-here-are-6-things-to-learn-from-cold-war-attempts-to-change-regimes /

nature of US policy. Indeed, it is essentially a continuation of the actual European policy, with the big difference that the European version is cynical, but noticeable, without the mask of preaching democracy and a new order.

The Truman Doctrine of 1947 is directed against the spread of Soviet influence in Iran, Turkey and Greece. In 1953 in Iran, the democratically elected government of Mohammad Mossadegh was overthrown. The American misunderstanding of the whole region of the Middle East as politics, society and culture dates back to these events and continues to the present. In 1952 President Eisenhower came to power, appointing anti-communist hawks John Dulles as his secretary of state and his brother Alan Dulles as CIA chief. Allowing the nationalization of the oil sector in Iran contradicts American and British interests. An oil embargo has been imposed, leading to an oil crisis and fears of a possible Iranian rapprochement with the Soviets, but equally with the oil interests and Iran's strategic position, led to the "Operation Ajax. Politicians, the army, the police and the clergy have been bribed with millions of dollars to actively oppose Prime Minister Mossadegh. The coup led to the establishment of a dictatorship of Shah Mohammed Reza Pahlavi. In the long run, the intervention in Iran and the lack of understanding of regional specifics will play a bad joke on Washington. Lack of cooperation in President Carter's team between the Secretary of State Cyrus Vance and Security Adviser Zbigniew Brzezinski will lead to an inadequate response to the protests and the ongoing revolution. With the fall of the Shahin Shah and the rise of Ayatollah Rukhollah Khomeini in 1979, the United States lost an essential strategic point forever, both geographically and economically.

Turkey becomes the second victim of Washington's foreign policy barbarism. In the context of socio-economic difficulties, on May 27, 1960, 38 Turkish army officers spearhead a coup to overthrow the Democratic Party government. The officers are part of the staff trained in 1948 from the U.S military to be a kind of "sleeping cell" in order to carry out a future coup. The successful coup was led by Colonel Alparslan Turkes and Gen. Jemal Gursel, who held the post of President of Turkey. The military junta fires from work and duty more than 230 Turkish army generals, more than 3,000 officers, 500 judges and prosecutors, and more than 1,000 university professors who do not share the views of the coup plotters. The May coup is not the last successful military coup in the country, but it is at the root of long-term political instability.

The CIA is financing the far-right organization "Sacred Connection" with 1 million dollars a year, entering directly into the Greek Civil War. US interests preclude the possibility of power being in the hands of governments that would allow normal relations with the Soviet Union. An example of a politician who is not a communist, but shows reason and thought for Greece, in relation to its interests, but not reflected through the interests of Washington, is George Papandreou. The CIA is also worried about the figure of his son, Andreas Papandreou, a Harvard graduate who heads a department at the University of Berkeley and has returned to Greece to work for the state. A declassified document from the US Embassy in Greece states that if Andreas Papandreou is elected, he will *significantly reduce military spending"* and 'will *distance Greece from NATO."* Of major interest is the announced conversation between President Lyndon Johnson and the Greek

Ambassador to the United States, Alexandros Matsas, during the Cyprus crisis. Johnson intervenes to resolve the dispute between Greece and Turkey, but it is interesting how he defines the situation: *"Fuck your Parliament and your Constitution. America is an elephant. Cyprus is a flea. Greece is a flea. And if these two fleas continue to bite the elephant, they will be hit by the elephant. Heavily struck. We pay a lot of US dollars to the Greeks, Mr Ambassador. If your Prime Minister keeps talking to me about democracy, Parliament and Constitution, he and his government will not last long."* At the end of 1966, it seems that the election in May 1967 will be won by the Centrist Union, Papandreou's party. Such a development would be against US interests. The result is the organization of a military coup, the so-called military junta, and the coming to power of an authoritarian regime led by Georgios Papadopoulos. It turns out that Johnson's words have been turned into action. After the military coup, thousands of communists were thrown into prisons, including without trial or sentence, and the "democratic" government began the mass use of torture on prisoners. George Papandreou dies under home arrest. Four of the five officers who took power on April 21, 1967, are very closely associated with the CIA and the United States. If it is assumed that Papadopoulos has been funded by the CIA, he is the first agent to become Prime Minister of a European country. The US government takes only a week to officially recognize the dictatorship and present it as a "legitimate democracy."

A retrospective look at the bipolar opposition to the Cold War serves as a starting point for analysing events after its end. Ironically, the good has already won, and it's time to establish the new *pax Americana*. The time when the temple of the god Janus closes its doors because the victor has returned to Rome.[34] The irony of the story is that chaos actually ensues whenever the opportunity for complete peace is provided and reached. In this example and model, the victorious state, which won the Cold war is the one that creates the new chaos in its own world order. The lack of a clear civilizational mission of the new world and the needs of the military-industrial complex outline the only particular parameter of the time after the Cold War – more uncertainty and more conflicts. The fear of a possible Soviet supremacy is replaced by a number of smaller fears. Firstly, as the awakening and growth of a new state entity to challenge the hegemony, but also the task of mastering the recently opened space that is being liberated and with the collapse of the Soviet system. The chaos brought from the United States to the world in the late 20th and early 21st centuries is characterized by several features. Purposeful and methodical attempt to liquidate the robust and national state at the expense of the corporate interests of the supranational corporations. It is changing the traditional views of the family and its model, built by mother and father, as the basis of every state and nation. Once changed and crippled the smallest cell of the society will again lead to the disintegration of a united, homogeneous state. An indefinite society cannot build a definite, healthy state. To facilitate the process of disintegration of

----

[34] In the Roman pantheon of deities, the god Janus is represented not only as the patron saint of farmers, but also as the patron saint of the new beginning. As well as those who go to war to return victorious. During the war, the doors of the temple remained open, and closed when the victor returned to Rome. Octavian Augustus officially closed the doors of the temple of Janus three times, as a symbol of complete peace – pax Romana. - author's note

states, it is necessary to erase the reflex carried by historical experience and historical memory. With this purpose, the already discussed distortion of history is taking place. Creating chaos leads to a world where the only rule is not to follow the rules. The listed parameters find their physical manifestations in economic, political and military aspects. The unpunished crime of imperial interests best expresses itself in a series of conflicts that have been going on for 20 years. Again, it is unnecessary to list all the encroachments on countries and economies to form a model, but on the contrary, a model is created by bringing out those that stand out as a scale of cynicism, brutality, and, accordingly, propaganda saturation.

With the end of the Cold War, disintegration processes begin in Southeast Europe with the disintegration of Yugoslavia. The major state, created after the First World War, turns out to be highly inconvenient for the United States. The well-known business model in the United States of buying large companies and selling them in small parts without creating a quality product, as a result, can be an excellent and cynical example of action against other countries. It is much easier to organize small, extremely dependent state entities according to someone else's will than a homogeneous state. The Balkan Peninsula has always been Europe's "gunpowder barrel," but in the late 20th and early 21st centuries, it has been used for Washington's interests, where the explosions are controlled and targeted. The model is the same as the one seen in the Colour Revolutions and the coup in Ukraine in 2014 – conflict in the periphery or heart of Europe means instability and a lever of control. Conflicts that are created with the purpose to remain unresolved. Wounds that are deliberately opened to be hurtful for both sides – the EU and Russia.

I dwell on a specific moment in the Yugoslav Wars, which outlines everything described so far as the cynicism of the Realpolitik. But it also goes much further as brutality. In February 1998, the Kosovo war began, which NATO and the United States describe as a war of independence. The war between the army of the Federal Republic of Yugoslavia and the terrorist organization Kosovo Liberation Army is an exact example of the illustrated model of creating hotspots in Europe. At the dawn of the new century, CIA funding from the KLA became known, and the agents' confessions that parts of the terrorist organization were trained by the US secret services. The deliberately provoked conflict is nothing new but corresponds to the operations already listed in the 1950s and 1960s. Another key aspect is the use of war as an occasion for NATO intervention. The operation, which shows the world unequivocally the end of the idea of "soft power", is called the "Noble Anvil" at the American headquarters. Organized and conducted without the consent and resolution of the United Nations, the American (and NATO) operation is an example of the abuse of power and force, the desire to test new and use old weapons, the famine of the military-industrial complex and a country as a whole, that has no long-term idea of its positive projection in the world. The popular phrase "elephant in a glass shop" corresponds to the metaphor of the elephant and the fleas of Lyndon Johnson to the Greek ambassador in 1963. Even if the intervention of NATO and the US military in this conflict can be seen as acceptable, despite the impossibility of such notion, the scale of the intervention is absolutely impossible to be justified.

The lack of an objective assessment of the human and moral dimension shows not only barbarism in action but also an unquenchable thirst for teaching a painful lesson to anyone who does not want to choose between the carrot and the stick but tries to follow his own path.

The bombing of Yugoslavia started on March 24, 1999, and lasted until June 11. The harsh statistics briefly show that in the first 4 hours of the operation alone, more than 100 rockets have been fired, and dozens are guided by satellites. The operation destroys not only Yugoslavia's military-industrial infrastructure, which is essential, but far higher and more important is the human cost, equivalent to atrocities. On the second day of the Orthodox Easter, April 12, 1999, a moving train is targeted the Gardelichka gorge. A rocket is fired, and it hits the train successfully. The American command defines the strike as a mistake. One missile can be considered a mistake. But after the first, there is a second one, and after it two more. If the use of a single rocket can be explained, even if it was not a passenger train, then the following 3 are only a sign of extreme brutality and a thirst for supremacy. But what does it mean to project superiority over an enemy who cannot defend themselves, as the case is with train passengers? The commander-in-chief of NATO troops in Europe (1997-2000), Wesley Clark, cites the excessive "speed" at which the train is moving and the coincidence that it is right on the bridge, which has been supposed to be blown up by them.

The forcible division of a country, followed by the model of "blue helmets", and subsequently the recognition of a new state, without ratification and against UN resolutions, creates a dangerous precedent that ultimately puts the world in a state of unpredictability. Good order and good peace are linked to the continuity and predictability of states and leaders. The only continuity that can be seen and analysed in the behaviour of the United States after the end of the Cold War is the creation of a model for identifying hotspots, conflict points not only in Europe and the post-Soviet space but also wherever there is an energy interest – oil reserves or a key transitional territory. It is the other peculiarity – if the intervention in Yugoslavia is conditioned on the one hand by the strategic importance of the region for the creation of a Balkan corridor and the restriction of the so-called Russian influence, but also as a geographical location for the transition of energy projects. The depth of the reasons lies in the rule that at the heart of any conflict in modern times, and creating a hot spot, is an energy project, whether it is about deposits, extraction or transit, and sometimes all three.

The adventurism and the sense of impunity and energy greed led to the organization of the Arab Spring in 2011 and dethroning some of the leaders that Washington, had appointed decades earlier. Interestingly, the use of NATO as a continuation of US foreign policy is essentially a hollow structure, a bureaucratic machine that, without the leading state, cannot even be considered genuinely combat-ready. The intervention in Libya in 2011 confirms this and gives grounds to be observed and analysed over time. In essence, NATO has three fully combat-ready armies – the American, the French, which is the only one in the EU with its own real military-industrial complex, but also a complete nuclear triad, with huge potential, and finally – the Turkish one. The intervention in Libya began on March 19, 2011, but less than a month later, on April 15, an article appears in the Washington Post with the headline that the bombs of the European command are over. The organization turns out to be practically incapable of conducting long-term military operations, and it comes down to this that NATO's European command should request the United States for more ammunition. It is happening against a country that has virtually little power to defend itself. Over time, this process deepens. The removal of Muammar Gaddafi, the breakdown of tribal consolidation in Libya because of the country's energy value will make the region unstable for a generation to come.

Two processes, within a few years, show the decline in the perception of the United States by the so called international community and proved to be, in the end, part of the last barriers to the final breakdown of the idea of a unipolar world. The war in Syria and the attempt to overthrow secular leader Bashar al-Assad proved to be a necessary process in the development of international relations in order to show several essential characteristics. On the one hand, the international, primarily European, community is still strongly influenced by American force diplomacy, but the crack is a fact. At the end of March 2018, President Trump has publicly announced that the United States will withdraw its troops from Syria, an action that his advisers have described as too spontaneous and unmeasured. Indeed, a week later, the United States accuses Assad of using chemical weapons against his own people in the city of Duma, Syria. A week later, in mid-April, the US military fires 103 Tomahawk missiles at various strategic sites in Syria. It happens without waiting for a decision of an expert commission by the UN, without inspections and analyses. The threat to the interests of the military-industrial complex results in an immediate reaction, regardless of the legality of the act. The trampling of the democracy but also of the choice of the American electorate shows that the country is ruled by several groups and their lobbies; and by its nature, the true power can be defined as supra-presidential. The strike on Syria in April 2018 is somewhat symbolic as a military result, but it creates conditions for further discreditation of Washington's foreign policy. The true purpose of those operations reveals itself as a photo negative - the thirst of the military lobby and companies for fresh conflicts to bring fresh money, but with the smell of oil. Two years after the barbaric act and the withdrawal of US troops from Syria, there are still troops, but to protect the oil wells. The occupation status of the US army is important to be noted, as there is no official call for help from the legitimate Syrian government. Russian and Iranian units both have invitations from the Syrian state.

The second process in recent years, which has shaped the pattern of the American decline on the international stage, is the attempt to create a civil war in Venezuela and overthrow the legitimate government by organizing a coup in 2019. Venezuelan oil and Venezuela's gold reserves proved to be very appetizing. The fear of non-American influence in Latin America provoked the citation of the Monroe Doctrine of 1823 by Donald Trump's national security adviser, the hawk John Bolton. After some months of horizontal and vertical attempts to overthrow the power in Caracas eventually lost central media coverage, and Washington quietly stopped talking about it. Venezuela is neither Iraq nor Afghanistan, and if there had been a military intervention, it would look more like Vietnam as an outcome. The

US found itself alone, and there are united Russian-Chinese interests against it. The only loyal ally that remained was Britain. The case of Venezuela has shown that the United States is not what it used to be. The positions of the American president no longer sound like infallible postulates. The promises of a new world worthy of the deaths of thousands of innocents can no longer serve to make sense of the cruelty of a force that fanatically believes in its hypocritical ideal. The moral and ethical path of the United States already has one direction that leads to decline.

§ 3. *The United States upon decline*

History has shown that the end of empires never happens instantly but can last for years or decades. The more technology advances, the exchange of data and the world "grows smaller", the faster historical time accelerates. During the life of a single person one could experience a lot of turning points and changes. A man who survived the horrors of World War II had to adapt to the world of the Internet. And the young man, who grew in the nineties and spent his teenage years in the first years of the 21st century, who is used to living without restrictions and without self-discipline, had to put his life in order within a month because of the global pandemic of the coronavirus COVID-19. The processes in the countries are similar. The time for adapting to the processes and events is greatly reduced. Different empires leave the world stage at different times and pace due to the inability to adjust and adapt to the conditions. And as a rule – the bigger the empire is, the more cumbersome it is, despite the fact that it is the basis of a particular process. In ancient times, such an empire was the Roman Empire, which succeeded to make a continent to be linked by a network of roads, which is essentially a small globalization. Its successor, the Eastern Roman Empire, continues this process, as the recent studies indicate that Byzantine artefacts from the mid-6th century can be found from Mali in West Africa to Tanzania in South Africa, numerous artefacts in India, China, and even Japan and Thailand. The role of the United States in modern times is similar, as a successor of the British Empire in accelerating globalization.

The time that took the British Empire to realize its new place in international relations and the lost status of great power is from World War II to the Suez Crisis of 1956. Under the Ottoman Empire, for example, the process lasts too long. Europe's "sick man" is beginning to feel weak as the stage of expansion comes to a halt. The impossibility of adaptation and adequate self-realized reforms gradually lead to complete dependence on the already very advanced technologically, administratively and militarily Western countries. The Ottoman Empire is artificially kept as a single united state so as not to disrupt the flow of money and resources to the West. Even further back in time, the Roman Empire begins its end when it commences to be surrounded by walls. No wall cannot be overcome by the turbulent times, giving birth to more and more turbulent nations. It is one of the most apparent signs of a downward trend in changing the status of a country. In particular – the moment when it begins to build physical or metaphorical walls—explained as a model – the moment when the state stops adapting to the conditions that it has created itself, or those that others import as nuances. When adaptation stops, or more precisely for the empires – when they cease to be the adaptive factor, the observer can assume that the empire has reached its peak and the path leads to decline.

The internal economic and social explosion that lead to the claim to participate in world affairs 100 years ago is currently having an impact on America's presence on the international stage, but with a negative sign. The explosion turns into a crisis. A crisis on all levels of American reality.

One of the significant issues, which has not yet reached its peak of growth, but will continue to develop, is replacing the professional principle with a quota in any horizontal and vertical structure of power. This model has been successfully transferred from the United States to Europe, and there are even attempts to impose it as a leading requirement. It is about replacing the meritocratic principle in selecting a person for a given position who is capable of performing a particular activity through his qualities, character, and education. The impersonal meritocracy that works in the United States and creates the conditions for building the image of a "land of unlimited possibilities" is deconstructed at the expense of the same neoliberal model that replaces the notion of the traditional family and gender. It is about the quota principle, false tolerance, accepting the "other" at the expense of the qualities of the capable one. The lack of awareness of this problem, even by the majority of the American analysts, or the conscious change of focus means that the more the fan of society unfolds, the less is the clarity about the chosen path. If the elite realizes that there is a problem with institutions and democracy, and even with the conduct of elections, it is in the entirely wrong direction. The definition that institutions cannot capture change in society is not just false but deliberately manipulative. Fukuyama rightly defines institutions as stable, repetitive patterns of behaviour that persist beyond the leadership of individual leaders. The problem arises when institutions fall victim to a conjectural model that proves to be problematic and even harmful. Most American analysts describe the electoral environment as positively developing because of the successful diversification of the political landscape. In the midterm elections of 2018, the renown edition Foreign Affairs, which serves as a guide for many observers, describes the new congress as "the most ethnically and racially diverse"[35], noting the presence of a number of men, women, people of colour or gay representatives. Such a breakdown is, in its essence, even offensive and discriminatory, rather than unifying and showing the good development of a society. The quota principle, starting from high levels of government, extends to every part of life, including culture. Even the prestigious once "Oscars" awards for film art turned out to be flawed by such practices if one pays attention to what products and on what basis they receive awards. There was even an influence on popular literary authors, who, by adapting their books written in the 1990s for theatrical productions, changed the racial traits of their characters to fit successfully into the quota model of society.[36]

---

[35]https://www.foreignaffairs.com/articles/united-states/2019-06-11/its-institutions-stupid

[36]In 2015 the author of the best-selling series of books in the world "Harry Potter", J. K. Rowling, practically changed the skin color of one of the three main characters in the series. The first book in the series was published in 1997, when the quota principle was still absent from political discourse. - How JK Rowling Feels About Hermione Changing Races In The Harry Potter Sequel,

Even more profound is another example, again related to the intellectual aspect, but directly affecting the nation's future – its children. Attention has already been paid to distorting history as a tool for exerting psychological influence in Europe and the world, but now it is directed inwards towards a nation. Erasing the collective historical memory and replacing it with fictional superheroes or studying the biographies of music performers is a sure sign of a deliberate error in the system. The removal of historical figures monuments from university courtyards and public parks is a direct encroachment on the memory of a nation. It is no coincidence that such a process of denying the past, by forgetting it, has been supported and encouraged in Europe. The closest case is the removal of various Soviet-era monuments in Ukraine after the 2014 coup. In the American scenario, we witnessed a petition organized in 2019 by students to remove a monument of President Thomas Jefferson because he has been a "slave owner and therefore a racist."[37]It is not an isolated case to be considered an incident; on the contrary – similar events have occurred in at least a few different states. Does this mean that the Declaration of Independence written by Jefferson must also be abolished? Erasing the truth and replacing it with convenient, unpretentious and impersonal information is the most direct way to the long-term mutilation of a nation. Once a society as a whole (including that part which must be corrective, namely the

---

https://www.cinemablend.com/pop/How-JK-Rowling-Feels-About-Hermione-Changing-Races-Harry-Potter-Sequel-106567 .html
[37] Thomas Jefferson statue fight about seizing government,
https://www.washingtontimes.com/news/2019/apr/2/thomas-jefferson-statue-fight-about-seizing-govern/

intellectuals) loses its reflexes to oppose influences that will contribute to its disintegration, it goes to the abyss. The replacement of ideas and qualities by quotas based on racial opposition, or the imposition of an artificial social order, the rise of artificial sexual diversity contrary to biology, speaks unequivocally of a crisis of spirit and will be understood only when it reaches an explosion point and a point of no return. The intangible dimensions of the crisis of spirituality receive their material manifestations.

Another problem that lies entirely in the plane of the material is the crisis of social inequality. The absence of a welfare state in the United States and the constant state of war outline the following picture of American society. The total wealth of citizens and non-governmental organizations in the third quarter of 2019 is $ 107 trillion. If it is distributed on average among all, it would mean that each family should have more than $ 800,000. Reality, however, shows a different picture – 50% of society and its lowest stratum own $ 1.67 trillion, or 1.6% of the total. At the same time, the wealthiest 10% of society owns 70% of these 107 trillion. Since the end of the Cold War, every year means opening the scissors of inequality, where the wealthiest 1% of American society steadily increases their income and wealth. At the same time, the poorest 62 million families lose every year. The rich get richer, and the poor get poorer. The Stanford Centre for Inequality Research shows statistics on the presence of 750,000 Americans who are virtually homeless, as people in active age from 31 to 50 predominate and military veterans.[38] These harsh statistics show the true face of the "American dream" and its wear and tear since the Cold War. The country of unlimited possibilities turns out to be a stepmother for its own population while preaching the protection of human rights abroad. If we use the artwork *"If U.S. land mass were divided like U.S. wealth"* of the American artist Stephen Ewan as an example to distribute the territory that the different groups of the society could own, the picture acquires an even harsher, grotesque look.[39] The states from Washington in the north to California in the south and all the way to Iowa would be owned by the wealthiest 1% of Americans. For the remaining 9%, the other half remains from Iowa to the Atlantic coast, 30% would own the Southern States, 20% the state of Texas, and the poorest 40% could afford the county around San Antonio, Texas. All these internal features, when combined with the accumulation of a huge external debt, insolvency, and the free printing of money, provoking their devaluation, lead to the creation of crises. Although declining, the giant radiates an influence that can still be called global in its nature. And this way, any created global crisis forces the rest of the world to pay for America's domestic and foreign needs.

The state of public intellectual and mental health is clearly shown by an example from 2020, after the declaration of the coronavirus COVID-19 as a pandemic by the WHO. Before

---

[38] https://inequality.stanford.edu/publications/20-facts-about-us-inequality-everyone-should-know

[39] Stephen Ewan, "If U.S. land mass were divided like U.S. wealth", 2013

introducing national measures for dealing with the pandemic, the first reflex of American society was to militarize further. Within days, weapons sales and permit applications jump 300%. March 2020 was the second most massive weapons purchase period (after the primary school shooting in January 2013) with almost 2 million sales. While China builds hospitals, in the United States are queues in front of gun shops. No spiritually mature and healthy country, especially the society that builds it, would allow the first to buy weapons during a viral pandemic. Lack of preparedness, due to the error of the education system as well (which in essence has been transferred as a model in European countries for years), easy panic, and subsequently the inability to self-discipline are markers of the true state of the nation. The question is, what will happen if the American citizen does not pay for his social package, especially in a state of a global pandemic or other type of crisis? Not even the mentioned one of COVID-19, but a hypothetical one in the future. The lack of affordable general health care will put a vast number of people at direct risk. But no one could answer the question of what would happen to these 750,000 virtually permanently homeless people. In order to illustrate the internal state of the country in even more detail, it is necessary to mention another extremely important component. I have already noted that every great empire lasts as long as it can logistically ensure its full existence. The condition of the road infrastructure in the United States is deteriorating every year, and maintenance funds and their insufficiency; it turns out that they cannot solve the problem in its entirety. Much of the state's infrastructure, including large industrial sites such as dams, major high-level road junctions in metropolises, etc., dates back to the Cold War and even earlier. The efforts to maintain world order after 1989 put them in a state of neglect of their own inner state. The annual reports of the American Society of Civil Engineers each year confirm the same conclusion – the state of infrastructure in the United States – from airports and ports to bridges, dams and roads – as estimated always vary between medium and extremely poor, according to the American rating system – between D- and C+. It is calculated that by 2025. $ 4.5 trillion[40] is needed to improve the network's condition, but not for its full restoration. The task facing American presidents will become more and more difficult for solving, and the answers and options for solutions will remain in the field of dialogue and controversy. Once again – the internal content does not match the external form. The claim for world hegemony, which comes with the end of the Cold War, turns out to be built on a weak foundation on the shoulders of a society that has not completed its own development. It, combined with the actions of American presidents and their foreign policy teams, has led to a gradual loss of confidence in the world community and, worse, to the development of anti-Americanism in even Western Europe and Asia. After removing the mask of the good policeman and world gendarme, the time of the brute force comes and the destruction of order in many countries, leaving chaos and ruins. The young empire finds itself without strong enough nerves to continue the demagoguery. The end result of the United States as growing to the number one power in the world has happened on an

---

[40]America's infrastructure is decaying - here's a look at how terrible things have gotten, https://www.businessinsider.com/asce-gives-us-infrastructure-a-d-2017-3

unprecedented scale in history, and this will be the basis for the long agony that lies ahead. However, the broken paradigm for a unipolar world offers opportunities for the United States to remain in the field of global relations as a significant part of the whole puzzle. The question will be whether they will be able to run at the speed of the new historical time, finding means and ways to adapt. The world is on the verge of establishing a new model that will build new security architecture.

3

Security Parameters in the Post-American World Order

§ 1. Risks and opportunities for the new security architecture

The United States has shown that a state or model can be universal only if it has the synthesis of a mass culture that is supported and spread through the methods of capital, and all this is ensured by a solid military presence. History offers only one such chance to turn a culture into a world one. The specific case of America is exceptional in its scale because, at the end of the Cold War, there was no other force that could oppose its power. However, the time from 1989 to 2020, these 30 years, which for history are a moment, are irretrievably wasted by the elite of the strongest country in the world. The achievement (both positive and negative) lies in the fact that a generation born in the late '80s and up to 2000 grew up entirely under the influence of this great power. Their whole lives will be influenced by language, culture, spirituality and needs, imposed mainly by the US model. It is the time that has created a significant part of weak people, some call it the "lost generation", who doesn't recognize spirituality as a high value, but on the contrary – perceive the fast life, exposed to all through social networks. The personal, intimate is somehow reduced to primitive sensations. The people's weakness also lies in the easy and absolute staggering of the temptations of this late capitalism, presented as progress and development. In the name of the feeling of "more", everything is often due to devotion to others, evoking the most declining instincts in people. In essence, the current situation, especially the so-called western culture, can be compared with the late Roman time of the vomitoriums – a separate hall in the villas and palaces, designed for vomiting the food which has been already eaten. The insatiable greed and desire to prolong the pleasure leading to abuse find the grotesque solution in the forced vomiting – by inserting a feather or hand into the throat. The decline of a state or system is first manifested by the signs of decline in society, mostly moral rather than economic. The present offers a similar picture of a weak society immersed in its own hedonistic reflexes. On the positive side, weak people will create difficult times, eventually giving birth to strong people. The irony of history is it being cyclic because strong people will create easy times.

Over the centuries and with the advancement of technology, history has begun to race faster and faster. Centuries turn into decades, and decades come together over several years. It is difficult for societies to comprehend the pace of development and realize their own insignificance or greatness within historical time. In the same way, the great projection of societies – states and unions find it difficult to realize their own role and the responsibility they bear for developing the new world. In the 21st century, history is running faster; the information flows that flood countries and individuals have no known analogue so far. It made people extremely informed about the present and isolated them from the instinct to learn from the past. The more daily information is received, the less time is spent looking into the recent and distant past. The thirst for knowledge has been massively replaced by the thirst for information in this natural, historical path of the growing possibility of exchanging news. Or more precisely – the thirst for the necessary and desired daily dose of information, in a state resembling addiction, but at the level of the mind. In the first fifth of the 21st century, people have become more alert but more easily manipulated. Numerous channels for obtaining information were adequately used in creating a model of a society that, in its sense and pursuit of freedom, fell into slavery. Financial dependence, credit life, controlled information in the mass media is part of the peculiarities of modern life.

For their part, states, as an enlarged model of human relations, have gone and are going through a similar path. In the upper class of world powers, there have been bullying states and others that are oppressed. Some formed a group of "cool" who set the standards for decent living, while others were forced to comply if they wanted to stay in the club of the cool. Whether forced directly or from a sense of backwardness and isolation, always with the same result. Behaviour that is analogous to human nature – the stronger to determine how worthy the other is to maintain a relationship with him. To achieve the desired level of coolness, some have lost themselves, becoming part of the so-called International community. This term is used to represent the whole world but represented only by a group of Western countries led by the United States. The concept of "international community" has three paths in the emerging new security framework collectively referred to as the security architecture. It must either disappear from mass use because of the considerable damages it has managed to inflict on both the material and the ethical world of truth and justice; or the second option is to acquire a new meaning, but when something new is created, it is best not to dress in an already compromised package. The third is related to the first one – dropping the concept of the preferred forms for describing the relations between individual state entities and replacing it with a new term that is not a product of hypocritical relations based on the interests of one or two countries. Exactly, the so-called International community organized the start of the war in Iraq in 2003, based on the lies of the elites of two states. Afterwards, it organizes the Arab Spring, opening Pandora's Box in the Middle East and North Africa for a long time to follow. It allows the participation of neo-Nazi's power in Ukraine, organizes many accusations against countries, accompanied by sanctions, without any evidence. As a leading representative of the bad, popular students among the countries, a personal goal of the United States has set itself the strategic task of stopping the North Stream-2 and its southern counterpart energy projects, despite Europe's economic need and justification. The intervention in Venezuela in 2019 and the coup attempt. Also, Washington's policy toward North Korea has failed, first on a psychological level, because it has failed to convince the world that Pyongyang is a threat to all of humanity. On the contrary, through the success of its rocket program, North Korea manages to achieve its goal – not to be a threat to humanity or the so-called "International community" but to defend its chosen model of civilizational development model. And it is its own people who decide whether it is good or bad, not to us, as Europeans. The rockets are for defensive purposes, not offensive. They gave Pyongyang that advantage that put negotiations with the United

States on an equal footing, and history loves audacity. All of these, as well as many other smaller examples, shape the general feeling of US foreign policy failure and, at the same time, greater activity on the part of other countries. As early as 2015, China had the ambition to overtake the United States by the amount of economic power. It also launched its long term project "One Belt-One Road", whose multi-vector nature, both geographically and as sectors, shaped the sustainable demand for competition in world affairs. Russia has managed to achieve something that no other country has achieved before – to be extremely well received by every country in the Arab world and at the same time to have a strong connection with Israel. The union with Crimea in 2014, the construction of bases in Tartus and Hmeim in Syria, and the successful keeping of Bashar Assad in power, despite the efforts of the US to bring him down, make Russia an unavoidable factor in the Mediterranean region. Examining these and all other processes put in order and discovering causal links creates a model that allows the provision of reasonable opportunities for the future of international relations. In "Sweet Thursday", John Steinbeck writes about the change as a light wind playing in the curtains at sunrise; that is, it comes gradually. But isn't discontent a catalyst for this change? – He continues. In this sense – the pattern of processes is not spontaneous; the explosion comes in stages, sometimes imperceptibly, accumulating over time and exploding at some point. For example, the accumulation of events and processes results in a gradual sense of change in the world order and affairs – the wear and tear of some countries and alliances, and the entry of new ones on the big stage, but certainly – a general feeling that the modelling of world politics comes from several different poles. The natural order and pace we have lived within recent years has shown that several more explosions of different scale are needed in a few consecutive years so that within the next five years the appearance of the new security architecture can be formed and the shape of the new political and cultural world be seen as accomplished. Again, the irony of history and time intervened to show the world how unprepared it has been for certain natural processes, but also, very importantly, how much it had done nothing to prepare itself. The light breeze in the curtains turned into a storm, which replaced the methodical, consistent change with experimental chaos within the time of months. The storm's name is COVID-19, the new coronavirus whose spread has gone through a phase of neglect followed by a state of chaos. Time will tell whether this is an experiment, gone wrong, a deliberately dropped experiment, or a natural call by nature to restore the balance in the world. So it remains for the mind to analyse and evaluate the changes which such a pandemic is causing to societies. The outbreak of the coronavirus and the panic it caused essentially set up a screen for another process that was expected and predictable. Already in the last third of 2019, there were signs of a coming economic recession – first in the United States and then in the rest of the world. An even more accurate term would be depression due to the projected scale expected for the first third of 2020. The economy of Western societies was suffocating because of its "overweight". If we assume that the economy has the form of a storage vessel, then its content goes beyond it. The high prices artificially maintained, aimed at satisfying financial capital, interest rates on loans, the ever-increasing ceiling on the US external debt, and many other factors foreshadowed that the contents would blow up the storage vessel that has a constant shape and volume. The government's goal in Washington was to maintain the feeling of economic growth until the end of the presidential elections in 2020. So in terms of the economy, the coronavirus pandemic proved to be an extremely convenient silencer and even a buffer that took the hit, and societies were successfully manipulated that the economic consequences were entirely due to the virus. No, the "overeating" of capital caused the coronavirus to germinate on "fertile" soil. In any case, this process replaced the smaller explosions in the course of world change and affected everyone. The pandemic is twofold in nature – first, it caused an economic depression, on the scale of the one in 1929 and second, as a social phenomenon comparable to the plague epidemic of the 14th century, but not in terms of the number of deaths. Still, the impact it has on society, such as fear, panic, and the current lack of knowledge on how to stop the spread. In today's world, it doesn't take years for the collapse of the existing order. The rapid course of history already discussed means that the scale of economic damage comparable to decades ago could be achieved in a matter of months but still could last and grow in the years to come. The agenda of society is rearranged fundamentally – even the news streams change their content. Until before the global panic attack with the coronavirus, "black" news(car or plane crashes, killing sprees, natural disasters etc) take up the first part of the streams, again due to consumer thirst, but also the bilateral, bordering on perverted, desire for something new, albeit negative. The background noise, which disturbs the citizen and keeps him in a constant state of anxiety and fear, has become a leading sense, occupying a central place in the picture.

Liking it or not, the 2020 coronavirus pandemic turns out to be a sobering factor, which first clearly and practically shows the shortcomings of the already outgoing security architecture in the world, including both the economy, the social sphere but also the well-known political connections and alliances. Second, it will most likely have a transformative character, and it is the catalyst for the changes that have already begun. A possible alternative is for the United States to try to restore the old format by force after the pandemic. Still, given the economic and social blow to the country, it would be suicidal. Within a month alone, the world's economies have been hit at all levels – logistics, manufacturing, employment. The whole sphere of services, namely this important part of the consumer society, turns out to be at a standstill. Within one week, the United States reported 6.6 million new unemployed, entering applications for benefits for the last two weeks of March 2020 with a total number of 9.95 million. In February 2020, a record low unemployment rate was reached for the last 50 years – 3.5%, equivalent to 5.79 million people. It means that within two weeks unemployment has jumped by almost 7%. In European countries, the picture acquires similar parameters – within a month, almost a million people in Spain have lost their jobs. For example, in Israel, whose population is smaller but the economy is traditionally strong, unemployment reaches 20%. It is very likely that entire sectors at the time of the pandemic have practically stopped and are in a state of coma – tourism, entertainment and restaurant business, and to a large extent, some industries. The reality of the pandemic is an indisputable fact, but undoubtedly certain subjects at the state and supranational level very quickly discover the opportunities provided by such a situation. Very soon after, the informational hyperbole and panic begin. Once started, a similar process begins to reproduce itself. The flow of information causes panic – first in society and then in the state and its leadership. The effect that is achieved in a case like this by creating mass panic, harnessing a natural pandemic is the real cause of trouble. When the state panics, it gradually stops the economic and social processes in an attempt to prevent proliferation, but in this way, it also stops the economy. It stops what gives sustainability – the production, and then only money remains. But then it runs out, and a collapse occurs, which would lead to printing more money with less value, then comes the inflation. The consumption stops. That is, the model is endangered, and the circulation of money stops. And even before that, as soon as the opportunity to run out of money is perceived, countries start turning to banks and debt funds. If governments do not act in this way, if they do not panic, they can immediately be accused of negligence. If they tighten the metaphorical leash too much, they become tyrants. And the whole vicious circle is dictated by the information environment and flows. Any government can be compromised too quickly in one extreme or the other, but the result will always be the same – it will enter the debt spiral. And in the case of the United States, $ 2 trillion was injected into the economy. A similar amount of money, corresponding to the annual budgets of several countries (for example, the annual budget of the United Kingdom for 2019 is about 1 trillion dollars), will have to be reimbursed in the near future. But this time, the world may not accept the role of saviour, paying for the crisis of one country. When money becomes the main commodity and the exchange of this commodity stops, it means a crisis and a collision of the so-called financial and industrial capital. It means that the time for reformatting the system has come. A possible risk is those whole sectors will change ownership and create a long-term dependence that is much stronger than the one before the pandemic.

In such a turbulent time, it will be easier for countries whose economies are based on sustainability rather than the principle of maximum profit to be preserved. The current clash at the energy level for oil price shows that the pandemic conditions do not stop the rest of the world processes. On the contrary, some processes may go unnoticed – such as small local wars at the regional level or the adoption of controversial legislation at the local, state level. The oil crisis is not a precedent, there have been several in the last 80 years, but there is currently overproduction leading to low prices. The tankers remain in the oceans, waiting for customers to appear. In these additional aggravating conditions, different countries will receive a different level of impact on their economies, and it will reflect in the near and medium future. The Russian oil industry can last 4-5 years if the oil price stays at levels of $ 15-25 or $ 30 per barrel (and even lower at certain times). And the state can handle that; however, the American industry cannot. This conclusion is confirmed by President Donald Trump. No sector will tolerate it. Healthcare will explode immediately because it is good, even excellent, but only for those who can pay. A significant portion of 30-40% of American society does not have or does not pay their social security regularly - what are they going to do? This issue will not change in one or two presidential mandates. This is a long-term problem, which is related to what has been written in the previous chapters, but also to the overall state of a country, which can drag the whole world behind it. There are three factors that keep the United States from these worst-case scenarios – the first is the vast gold reserve of over 8,000 tons, the largest in the world and equal to the total reserve of the following three countries on the list combined. The second factor is the American base of many of the strongest banks in the world, so the biggest clash between financial and industrial capital is in the US. The third factor is the enormous nuclear power, which is a deterrent to all the worst processes. It is the factor that saved Russia in the 1990s.

The pandemic of 2020 shows the readiness of the individual state and allied subjects to deal with challenges, what condition they will enter, and what influence they will have in the new structuring of the world. China was the first country that acted with a huge scope, but also the first one that manages to cope with the situation within two months and from a state of pause, to return to a relatively normal work process and even to be able to fulfil external orders for the delivery of goods again. Its exceptional ability to adapt to emergency conditions becomes apparent. A huge, and the most populous country, which suggests clumsiness, did precisely the opposite – the fastest sprint with a huge weight on the back. It happens due to several factors: First – the way of life and values in Chinese society, which is very different from those in the United States or Western countries and the whole Europe. One cannot neglect the important circumstance that historically the first state administration, which can be defined as modern, originated in China 3000 years ago.[41]A country where the centralization of power and the meritocratic administration precede the rule of law by a millennium proves to

____

[41]See Francis Fukuyama, Political Order and Political Decline.

work better in a crisis. Hence the modern form – the centralized state model, with clear responsibilities and dependencies, even under the fear of failure and the consequences after that – manages to adapt the entire state machine to the new conditions.

Russia is the second country, which reacts cautiously and reluctantly to the so-called "International community" messages, a concept whose meaning has already been clarified. The last 30 years have been crucial for Russia's economy, as the most important test for the state and its existence. From complete ideological, social and economic timelessness, the world has been shown that this country cannot be defeated from the outside, but only from the inside, due to its numerous objective specifics. The Russian economy has undergone many changes; it has learned, together with the state, how to function during several crises, which has made it sustainable. The experience after the collapse of the Soviet system and the situation where the citizens of one country in a moment find themselves in many other countries is a state of ordeal much greater than the 2020 pandemic; the challenges of the 1990s in the rapid looting and disintegration of the state, combined with the trials of the Chechen wars to preserve state consolidation. Then comes the global economic crisis of 2008, which finds the country in an unfinished state, but ultimately makes it stronger until the 2014 sanctions imposed by the United States and the European Union after Crimea's accession to the country. The last 30 years have proved to be the necessary difficulties for this country, probably undesirable, but is there a person who enjoys life's challenges. Initially, he accepts them as a weight and burden, but only after overcoming them realize that this is an experience that creates reflexes and instincts to deal with the following challenges of life. The same thing happens to Russia – it learns, along with the historical experience, to survive in a state of constant crisis, and even to grow and develop. It is the main factor in implementing a new security model in the world – to be presented by countries that have proven the ability to survive and adapt. Probably it will be the basis of the new socio-cultural model – the preservation of globalization in the field of culture and economy, but also returning to a higher level of culture. And it is likely to happen within a constant state of crisis in the world.

At the other extreme, among the examples of dealing with a crisis is Britain. In recent years it has shown a state that can be characterized by a few words: lack of direction, a state of laziness and chaos. The timelessness for this country begins with the mentality of its citizens – the stepping of old laurels, a well-established social system, producing a mass refusal to carry out many activities, provided to the migrants, against whom they later voted in a referendum, signal confusion, lack of dynamics and hence – prerequisites for fading the whole country. Once based on pioneering, daring, and a desire to grow, the old true greatness has been replaced by outright laziness, a residual arrogance that creates the preconditions for disintegration. Leaving the EU can be interpreted multilaterally – on the one hand as the instinct of a survivor leaving a sinking ship if viewed positively; choosing the Anglo-Saxon model as a civilizational order and finally attaching it to US policy; and a third, which can be combined with the second one – an irrational sense of difference with Europe and thus – a choice of the closest other ally. The future of Britain is likely to be in some form of disintegration – whether direct, into its constituent parts – Scotland, the reunification of the two Irelands, etc. or the formal stay in a common state trying for some time to balance between the EU and the US, through NATO and the huge financial influence it possess. Here is the battle of the United States and the EU – the opportunity the London based financial capital to be attracted by New York or Germany. If Britain loses this most important battle and war to preserve its financial heart based in London, it loses everything else by the domino effect. The financial centre in London is the key to the integrity of this country. In the long run, Britain's influence will certainly not increase; on the contrary – the decline will lead to a state of a middle European state, but for the understandings of the old empire, it also means a crisis of spirit. Most cynically said, history doesn't care about it. History is a cynical science, and historians can rightly be called cynics, so it doesn't matter for civilization whether this state will exist in its current form or not. The same applies and applied for many other countries. Its greatness remains in the past and can only provoke gratitude from the world, but even this is not certain; the world – like history, is also cynical, but also predatory. Only the most adaptive remain if a trace is sought in Darwin's teachings.

For years, there has been a growing Euroscepticism towards Brussels and the state of the European Union. For the sixth or seventh time in a row, the current attempt to unite Europe, but this time by peaceful means, turns out to be too optimistic, more euphoric, and less sensible. In the end, a product is obtained that looks like a large and strong predator but turns out to have cardboard teeth. As early as 2003, when the United States organized a coalition for the war in Iraq, the EU was divided. The United States has succeeded in attracting Britain, Italy, and including Eastern European countries, which have been quick to prove themselves worthy of an organization like NATO. Germany and France find common ground with Russia. American abuse of the EU is caused by the union's own weakness, factually and externally manifested. It doesn't take much for a true predator and the largest predator to smell weakness and take advantage of it. The responsibility is as much in the United States as it is in the EU and its inability to be what it wants. In a world of predators, it is impossible to survive only with declarations, programs and beautiful ideas; you need even a brutal manifestation of force. Over time, Washington's abuse of the EU has become more apparent – in essence, the EU has always been internally divided between the union of France and Germany on the one hand, Britain on the other, and the Baltic states and Poland on the third, which in their foreign policies turns into transmissions of Washington, a vast Trojan horse created with the enlargement of the EU to the East. Hence the established dependence – the enlargement of the EU is connected with the enlargement of NATO.

One of the biggest challenges for the EU has been the defence of its energy policy related to major gas projects with Russia. Washington's efforts to halt Nord Stream 2 have shown the importance of this project for both the EU and the United States. It becomes clear that for the United States, Europe is like a backyard in which Washington wants to determine relations with its neighbours. Gradually, efforts shifted from official letters to the European Commission, through diplomatic pressure, to economic sanctions and direct threats to countries and companies. Dealing with American anxiety on the two major energy projects from the north and south, however, shows that the cardboard-toothed predator could see the light in the tunnel of its existence. But no state or union entity grows to a complete form or reaches a final state – regardless of a positive or negative outcome – without moments and processes of trial. The idea of the existence of the European Union is too good to be without consequences. And the opportunity to build a strong relationship with Russia and fulfil the Eurasian dream is Washington's biggest nightmare. That is why all major local hotspots in recent years have found themselves in Europe, between the EU and Russia. However, the union may also squander its historic chance if it does not respond in a way that allows it to adapt to the dynamics of the modern world. Currently, the field for free movement is not large, as one of the levers of influence on the part of the United States is too powerful – the huge military personnel in the EU, located in different countries, at key locations and bases. The failure of US foreign policy on energy projects with Russia is primarily the result of a long process of self-discrediting of the United States worldwide and the loss of its position since the end of the Cold War. But failure in one direction does not mean release from influence; on the contrary – it will become stronger and more obvious. Gradually, the figure of the carrot will disappear entirely from the possibilities, and only the stick will remain. Exhaustion means that Washington's move is down, but in the meantime, Europe can take a lot of "discipline" through the functions of the stick.

The emergence of the coronavirus pandemic in 2020 may turn out, in the end, to be positive, from the point of view of the manifestation of the real condition of states and unions. The Western model of democracy seems to be an obstacle to developing and strengthening the state in times of crisis. The purifying factor of the crisis leaves the EU with several options for the future.

Starting from the negative to the positive possibilities, the first means the end of the EU in its current state. When even one internal state border is closed in a union based on the idea of freedom of movement, there is no union. It means that decisions are made again at the level of nation-states, and everyone manages on their own, regardless of the money that will be injected as aid from the central level. Such moments of the trial show the real state of a union or subject. It is clear that the EU is still too far from that significant and long-awaited idea of a common family. Probably it will never happen. The idea of a strong nation-state, which has long been presented as a negative narrative by many researchers, turns out to be extremely necessary. The awareness of seeking support in one's own national community and state has shown that Europe is much more than simply a modern entity, blurring the ideas of nationality, traditions, and even gender. Instinct made thousands of people to leave their countries of residence and work and return to where they were born. The era of economic and cultural globalism cannot replace the sense of security given by the place still called "home", even if it comes from the poorest state in a union. The worst-case scenario for the EU in the forthcoming reformatting is to break up into components that remain formally within the union, taking whatever they can until the time comes when the union's flag will be taken down, not only in isolated cases as in Italy or France but everywhere. Such a death would be a failure for the German and French idea of a common space uniting capital and people. The fact that the EU has failed to deal collectively as an alliance with the pandemic has reversed the repercussions of the collective national consciousness. A scenario of informal or real disintegration of the EU is extremely positive for Washington because it will simply create a whole corridor of direct official influence from the Baltic to the Black Sea. From the point of view of Russia, this is a negative scenario, in which it will be impossible to accomplish the Eurasian dream of a common economic space for a very long time to come. In the global puzzle, such a scenario will also be an obstacle to the Chinese "One Belt One Road" initiative, despite the idea that it is easier to work with countries per piece. In the general case, this is true, but not when there are American military bases on the territory of these countries, and the governments are directly dependent on the will of the democratic or republican elite in Washington.

The second possibility for the EU in the near future after the pandemic is again related to the rediscovery of the nation-state, but to use as a basis for a union built on a reasonable and pragmatic vision of mutual benefit and interdependence. The preservation of the common external borders of the union, returning to the free movement of people, but with respect for national identities and policies within a union based on pragmatism. The collaboration of national companies and research centres with one another related to sensitive and vital sectors in pan-European clusters – exchange of information, opportunities and progress. Indeed, in this scenario, each country will begin to re-evaluate, recognize and cherish its own staff and human resources, which will mean stepping up efforts to keep professionals within the nation-state by ensuring a better life; the revival of the national structures guaranteeing the national security of the countries – defence, energy, etc. Failure within a pandemic can be conveyed as an opportunity for failure within another type of conflict due to human relationships: war – physical, informational, and even biological. In short, the second option can be defined as a union of nation-states with strong economies and a shared common economic space, set in certain precise parameters, which most likely means a weakening of the headquarters in Brussels. Indeed, ways will be sought for each nation-state to be able to develop and work into a state of autarky in certain strategic sectors – from agriculture to defence (physical security but also informational and biological).

The third option allows a complete rethinking of the current state of the union, which led to the collapse at the most important time for handling the current crisis – its genesis. Not only a crisis related to a natural pandemic but any caused by the human factor, which threatens the union as a whole. It means recognizing the threat posed by NATO, despite its different nature but essentially suffocating the EU. NATO will always be a continuation of Washington's policy, no matter what will be the future scenario for the EU. For history, the EU is a young formation. The common currency is only under 20 years old, and enlargement in different years happens so fast, often too much and under pressure, that such a union cannot be sustainable. It has not had the necessary time to acquire homogeneity and strength. Countries can use their historical experience – both on their own, but mostly as intertwined historical relations over the centuries – to build a pragmatic foundation. Europe has a common collective memory that can lead to the birth of a truly mature subject if appropriately used. Otherwise, the battle for history will favour blurring and erasing the collective memory, which will lead to the repetition of all mistakes again.

The fourth possibility for the Union is mimicry of change. It is missing the lessons of the last ten years as moods, actions and strategies in the field of geopolitics and the pandemic of 2020. On a superficial level – an attempt at reforms again carried out through the prism of the Brussels bureaucracy. At the real level – some attempt of a synthesis between some of the previous possibilities – at the formal level – "change" in Brussels, at the informal level – the division of countries into visible blocs and the conduct of its regional policy of interests.

In any possible scenario, it is to be expected that, despite its declining influence, Washington will continue its silent war on both the information and economic levels. The following blows from Washington are logical to be on the European economy. First on Germany, but then on France. The first, because of its powerful economy and Nord Stream-2, and the second one – because of its own military-industrial complex, which is the only competitor from the Union, but also because of even loud declarations of a common European security space, with a joint European army that automatically excludes the American one. The military-industrial complex of France is a matter that may cause future problems in the US-EU relationship. But also the French recognition and respect for Russia's key role for the outcome of World War II. A position which opposes the long-running propaganda narrative of whose role is crucial in the liberation of

Europe from Nazism. The coronavirus pandemic occurs in a year when some of the most influential European leaders and politicians agreed to take part in the Victory parade in Moscow on May 9, despite the imposed sanctions and American reluctance. The pandemic eventually postponed and ruined the previous plans. At the moment, the integrity of the European Union rests solely on Germany and France and their determination to keep the EU alive and whole. Expressing with practical means the desired closeness to Russia is a sufficient motive for action at every level – economic, financial, and psychological. Through sanctions, interference in the internal affairs of other countries and judicial systems, and by distorting historical facts. Europe faces the challenge of maintaining its economic and financial strength, but just as important, its sense of Europeanism. And that, according to French President Macron, certainly includes Russia.

One of the great positive features of Europe is that it does not stop changing. It is the only place in the world where something has always been happening for 2,000 years. And with the acceleration of historical time, the intensity of events also increases. Europe is an unfinished form, but with the opportunity to rediscover itself. And this rediscovery definitely includes Russia, which is an integral part of the sense of Europeanism, albeit different in itself because of its vastness. To a large extent, a positive future for Europe – as a union, as a territory, economy and culture – is linked to Russia. It is no exaggeration to say that the EU needs Russia for its existence. The sooner the unavoidable historical and contemporary circumstance is realized that culturally Europe means the space from Lisbon to Moscow, the healthier it is for the continent's future. Umberto Eco rightly notes in an interview, without being quoted, first about the Middle Ages and then about the present – that if a man finds himself in Provence or another point in Europe and then goes to Baden or Bavaria, will still feel European and sensing Europe around. But if the same person finds himself in New York, he will face a space radically different from the European one. In any scenario for Europe, there will be an inevitable desire for reindustrialisation. Some political forces, accused in the recent past of being nationalistic or overly Eurosceptic, have linked their rhetoric and vision for reindustrialization for years. It turns out that it is inevitable that there will be no strong state control over strategic sectors for the existence of a state – security, energy, healthcare, education. It is even hypocritical to say the opposite when at the same time the strong countries have never denied this policy, and indeed do everything possible to buy out entire national sectors of weaker countries; to buy energy distribution companies, to buy concessions on mines, forests, ports, drug development companies, etc. History is not simply over or ended, but on the contrary – it will become more aggressive, along with its rapid pace, more ruthless, because at a time when the significance of an event lasts a day or two or a week, and the biggest – month or two, then oblivion lurks around the corner. And only societies that learn to run at the speed of the new historical time will find their worthy place in the future and build the new security architecture. All the others will be chewed and spit out by history and may not even be described with more than a page in future textbooks and history books.

When commenting on the new model of security in the world and Europe, there is no way not to pay significant attention to NATO in particular, and not as a general consideration among the possibilities. In essence, NATO is exhausted as an ideology – it is hollow. This is the shortest definition of this old ghost. After the end of the Cold War, its old arch-enemies, the Warsaw Pact and the Soviet Union disappear. The metamorphoses after 1989 are associated with the artificially finding of form and meaning, often against self-bred enemies. The organization is a direct continuation of Washington's foreign policy, and it is used as a bat, albeit a rubber one. Apart from the US, French and Turkish armies, all the others are just territories where US troops can be deployed. The fighting capacity of other countries is minimal. The described intervention in Libya in 2011 was needed to demonstrate such a statement. The Russian threat is a demon doll, brandished and instigated periodically to justify its own existence, most often by conducting training against a dubious anonymous enemy, initially disguised as international terrorism, against which missiles from European countries are aimed, until the announcement of Russia as an enemy. NATO will be as strong as the United States. The decline of the big giant will gradually weaken the organisation's influence, but we must remember the metaphor of the cat, which is pressed into the corner. It is most dangerous when it is stressed, frightened and at a dead end. The new security architecture in the world will set a fundamental challenge to NATO's existence.

European countries' awareness of Russia's illusory threat could also mean rethinking NATO's role. The role of Turkey, which plays a double and pragmatic game, is interesting. Simultaneously a member of NATO and one of the three combat-ready armies, but at the same time entering into a strategic, pragmatic friendship with Moscow. Turkey successfully fulfils its ambition to be an unavoidable regional factor – both in the field of energy and geopolitically. An acceptable opportunity is to achieve the ambition to possess its own nuclear weapons in the coming years. Erdogan's ideas for reviving the influence of the Ottoman Empire are directly related to Russia's blessing. The only person and political leader who has proven to be a deterrent to Erdogan and his ambitions is Vladimir Putin. And it may even turn out that the otherwise stable Erdogan may be directly dependent for his political future and existence on good relations with Russia. He is currently profitable and has remained in power even after the pro-American coup attempt in 2016. In the near future, there may come a time when he will be abruptly replaced in one way or another. A matter of pragmatism, the same that applies for the close relationship with Russia. But the issue is exceptionally historical. There is no other country to bring fear to Turkey but Russia. Historical memory creates reflexes of fear and respect. Thus, in the sustainable new world order, NATO may also be a formally existing organization but not a homogeneous source of security or influence. NATO is as strong as the United States can withstand. And the collapse of the United States may come from its weight and instability rather than from an external enemy The pandemic of 2020 showed another important circumstance – the idea of the necessary enemy, but from a Russian point of view. As the United States needs the figure of an enemy, the same can be said for a country like Russia. Russia's aid to Washington during a viral pandemic is more of a symbolic act, of course essentially the result of universal values, but with the clear awareness that it helps someone who sees you as an enemy. Again a manifestation of the imperial creative instinct, but already shaped through the virtue of charity, and not exclusively of pragmatic interest, free of passion and emotion. That is – grown, mature and ready to participate in the creation of the new security architecture. The scale of such humanitarian aid from Europe to America shows, and the replacement of weapons with medical supplies shows the previously established rule that no conflict in the world can be resolved without Russia's participation. The second sure participant in the already collective architecture is China. Consistent, methodical, especially arms-free, Chinese policy, economic power, demonstrated as labour productivity and innovation, discipline, and scope, define China as one of the poles of global relations. The interdependence of Russia and China defines them as current strategic partners, largely united by the presence of the same competitor. But the world cannot exist without opposition. It is at the heart of progress. Whether it is competition between people, companies, and the struggle for customers, or states and unions in their desire and contest of showing a better civilizational model is equal to progress. But it is always important not to halt dialogue, to maintain rivalry, but within limits and a frame. And that means – in times of need to help your enemy. The necessary enemy – you help to have it. Therefore, it is logical to admit the possibility that countries like Russia and China would save the United States from falling into a state of disintegration or ruin in order to maintain a sense of order. And the order is also expressed in the opposition. The order does not mean eternal peace. It is a dream that cannot exist because it contradicts human nature. Man is a civilized animal, but still, he cannot escape from his own nature, which makes him the most dangerous predator. The appearance of the new security model so far takes the form of a triangle at its core – the United

States, Russia and China, with the long-term advantage of the latter two. The best role is one of the balancer, which is both a part from the foundation but also a mediator. It is precisely Russia's new role – due to its geographical location, the demonstrated and proven maturity of foreign policy, and an example of imperial multi-confessionalism. A world organized on interdependencies, forming a delicate balance, but not excluding the possibility of even military confrontation. The three-dimensional architecture of security, in the form of a triangular multi-storey prism, and its foundation formed by United States-Russia-China, will give the long-term appearance of the modern, changing world.

§ 2. The changing world

The world we live in has known many oppositions over the years: civilization – barbarism; Christianity – paganism; democracy – communism; West-East, etc., but in this new time managed to mature and acquire a general character for the first time opposition of a new type: America – almost everyone else. One country, due to its unprecedented influence but also unprecedented greed, managed to achieve something that no one else has achieved – it has managed to gain the contempt and suspicion of all. It has happened consistently through time and not as a one-off event but took years. As a result, the experiment for the existence of a unipolar world failed. The world is already operating in a new framework – a triangular prism on many levels. It makes the three-dimensional architecture shape, with the processes happening between each point and each level running in parallel and simultaneously. We tentatively call each level "floors" to make it easier to visualize and comprehend. On the first floor of the figure are three countries – the United States, Russia

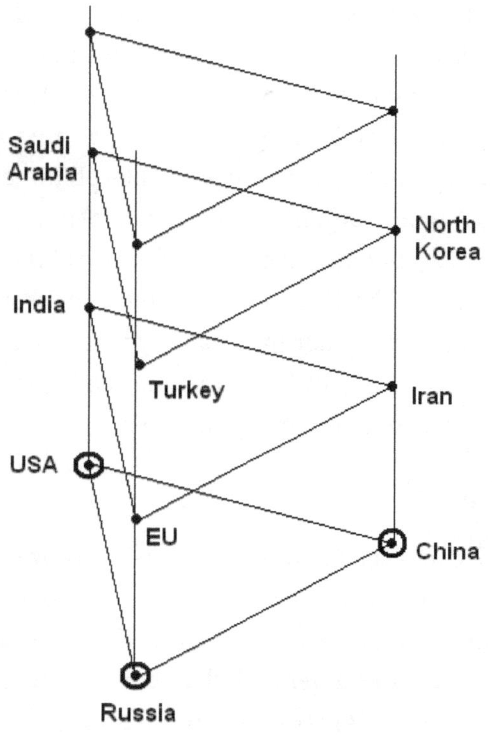

and China. The foundation is the essential part of this new frame, as it supports the whole structure from the bottom up, like a building. The more stable the foundation, the more stable the building. But the higher the floors, the more important all the other countries are because of the balance they carry. Each subsequent floor includes countries involved in global, regional or local processes. For example, the second floor may consist of the following three entities – the EU(and or UK), Iran and India. Third floor – Saudi Arabia, North Korea and Turkey. All existing bloc unions and organizations can be easily explained in terms of format and existence through the participation of one or more of the states at the core of the figure.

For example, NATO like a US functionary can be deployed as an organization in the three-dimensional space between the floors and the inclusive points, thus projecting the real power of the alliance. NATO includes one of the states from the foundation – the United States. It reaches as an influence to Turkey, which is a member, the EU countries, which currently have no real opportunity to secede, and Saudi Arabia, albeit indirectly. On the other hand, the force that opposes NATO consists of two main points – China and Russia, at the second level – Iran and partly India, at the third level – North Korea (which has successfully defended its own position, albeit isolated) and Turkey, whose role can be reasonably considered ambiguous. As explained, by applying in the three-dimensional prismatic space, NATO is at a disadvantage and is somewhat isolated. Unlike the old security model, a condition that has changed dramatically and deteriorated during and after the Cold War. In its current form, the EU occupies the second floor of the prism due to its rather regional nature and the inability to pursue a firm, unified foreign policy, despite high trade and economic performance. Dependencies at different levels in the prism make the EU unsustainable. After the 2020 pandemic, they make it uncertain as a whole, but it should be noted – the EU can occupy the floors close to the base only if some form of unification is preserved. In a physical disintegration, most countries will not even have a regional influence that extends beyond continental Europe or their close region. Still, the EU's position is key, similar to Russia's one, which is fundamental. Suppose Russia is a balancer of the three countries defining the base of the model. In that case, the EU is a balancer of the second level of regional powers, as Europe is always the most appetizing and desirable field of conflict. In one way or another, each of the basic countries needs the space of the EU and Europe. China – for its "One Belt One Road" project and the need for supplying its economy with an expanding market, the United States – the need for maintaining huge military personnel in Europe as a buffer against Russia, but also a field for operating its own transnational corporations. And Russia, which is continentally connected to the EU and China, is culturally similar to Europe but suffering from organized conflicts on the borders. The EU's role can be key, influencing both the base and the upper floors, if the chance that history will give is captured. Iran's location on the second floor of the three-dimensional prism, placed after China, close to Russia and the EU, could be explained by a number of factors. Iran is not just a random country. It is a 4,000 year-old culture, with an exceptional balance between science and religion, dozens of science centres, a nuclear state, and most likely a nuclear power. A key oil producer, but also a key territory for transit, and as the rule states – in the heart of any modern conflict lies an energy interest. A proper analysis should make it clear that if there is a country that would not actually be at war with Iran, it is the United States. Even in the events of 2019 and early 2020, linked to US-Iran relations, Washington's ultimate goal is to sit at the negotiating table. It proves that President Trump had a sense of conducting foreign policy along the edge of the blade – gambling, avant-garde, incomprehensible to the mass observer. But with the Pentagon's full awareness that war with Iran is, first, pointless and, second, that the enormous negative consequences for the US economy cannot be fully foreseen, at any outcome. Iran is a country which remembers history and builds upon it. Its role in the future of international relations will be key.

The processes in the world would not be complete without taking into account the influence and opportunities of another of the most ancient cultures and the country it embodies, namely India. There are four prerequisites for it to fall into the second level of the prism. But there is even the potential to be among the three countries creating the stability triangle so far without articulated ambition. The first prerequisite is the huge population, which is constantly growing. Ancient culture, traditions and the desire for education can be key factors. At the other pole, however, are the peculiarities and problems that prevent the accumulation of enormous national energy to harness the potential. The education system has serious infrastructural problems – physical lack of space, uneven funding, lack of technology, peculiarities of the family environment, high level of functional illiteracy and others. The considerable potential is also hampered by social inequality and a general sense of poverty. The second positive prerequisite for India to be among the most influential countries is its territory – first, it represents a whole subcontinent, standing in a key place in the world. A vast territory, which was not accidentally strategic to the British Empire in the past. The third prerequisite is the fact that the country is in the club of nuclear countries with a nuclear arsenal. India is also among the top 10 countries with the largest gold reserves, also with a tendency to increase its reserves, which by 2020 is over 600 tons. All these factors create the conditions for the country to fall into any future scenario concerning the reformatting of international relations. Currently, India cannot surpass its shadow of regional power because of the listed factors and its purely regional ambitions and problems.

Particular attention should be paid to a country that is too small to occupy any of these levels but is too large to be limited to one of them. The State of Israel is a small player with great potential. Extremely close to the United States, almost like docked vessels, but at the same time close to Russia, due to a large number of Russian Jews, citizens of Israel. It is no coincidence that before the elections in 2019, Israeli Prime Minister Netanyahu first met with Donald Trump in Washington, D.C., and flew to Moscow a few days later, where he met with Vladimir Putin. At the beginning of 2020, Putin attended an official unveiling ceremony for a monument to the victims of Nazism during the siege of Leningrad. Russian-speaking Israelis count about 770,000 out of a total of 6.3 million eligible to vote. The influence of the State of Israel is multifaceted – both at the level of history, due to the tragedy of the Holocaust, but also all periods of Jewish persecution in world history, at the level of politics and military power as well. Unofficially, but with a high dose of authenticity, it is assumed that Israel not only has access to its own nuclear weapons but has a complete nuclear triad. The combat capability and motivation of the Israeli army is probably at a much higher level than most countries in the world, certainly in the top 5 of combat-ready and efficient troops. Especially in 2019, it is clear that while the United States would talk about striking Iranian strategic targets, Israel could carry them out while Washington is still at the beginning of the talk. The State of Israel is the most accurate example of harnessing all available national potential in defending the idea of the right to live.

It is unnecessary to list and analyze all participants and processes with an already created model. By stepping on the established principle for shaping the three-dimensional architecture and knowing the peculiarities of a process or subject, it is possible to apply both vertically and horizontally in the space of the figure. It is important, however, to pay attention to a not so visible but significant feature, exerting its influence, without its obvious application. The existence of an opportunity in time to manifest a new form of alternative statehood, replacing the current perception of people, nation, state. We are talking about transnational corporations, which are still deeply entangled in the bodies of states. It is possible for entities such as Google, Facebook and Amazon and others to go beyond the capabilities of the country they come from, in their ability to restrain them, and to enter the field of geopolitics as an alternative to the state. A mega-corporation that will start offering its affiliates its own rules, its own insurance, entering deep into the personal space, and voluntarily by the citizens and the societies, organizing its own cryptocurrencies. And on the principle of organizing public events or protests to organize their own transnational army – by virtual or physical soldiers. Once imposed in an individual's life, such a form of alternative statehood can be far more dangerous than the traditional view of even the strongest state. An application launched as a means of communication can become a cancer that monitors every step of people's physical and mental life. From information about physical health, through access to bank accounts, to location detection, means absolute control. It is not even possible to prove that there is a way out due to the peculiarities of modern life. Even approaching such a scenario, related to the development of transnational corporations, requires traditional countries to build a reflex and a real protection structure. Such an example acquires a real form and content in Russia by creating a national Internet that can protect the country from hacker attacks and attacks on an intellectual level, but certainly a kind of protection against the already described new type of danger. The presented security architecture allows and shows as secure the possibilities of collision and attempts to change several different levels simultaneously. It means that there is a natural instinct to fight and the ambition to get closer to the base, and why not a future replacement of one of the base points with another. Relations between states are an enlarged model of interpersonal relations. All the examples so far in the text have transposed human qualities on the states, as they are built by people and are their likeness – with all their positive and negative features. That is why the process of confrontation and opposition is natural, but also the finding of balance. The discourse on the future passes within this model, and new and old contradictions about the world order and the regulation of human relations will take place in it. In addition to this new type of clash for humanity, on a virtual and transnational level, since the beginning of the 21st century, the old science-religion clash has been charged with new energy, especially with the emergence of the 2020 pandemic. It is clear that one part of the world has not yet learned to strike a balance between the two and has not realized that only through it the human progress as a race is possible. It was this fundamental clash that gave birth to successes in science, as an attempt to deny religion, but at the same time succeeding because of its pressure. The interdependence between reason and spirit underlies man himself as a natural creation. Religion in the individual, but also on a larger scale, often begins due to suffering. Man begins to seek salvation beyond his own knowledge when he finds no other way out. Societies seek salvation and support in religion when the collective sense of security is faced with the test of a natural disaster for which science is not ready yet to give a solution.

Science, on the other hand, works best when it has religion as a corrective, or in some past times as a judge and persecutor. The impetus for scientists has often been to prove the absence of divinity in the processes, when in fact the divine is proved through human achievements themselves. The infinity of the universe, constantly proven by scientists, must show people, through their own greatness, how insignificant they are against the background of the common. In a world that has proved through the actions of states and peoples that often what is seen on the surface as processes is, in fact, something different, even false, it means that no possibility of interpretation should be ruled out. Conversely, in the field of pragmatism, in the long run, the state entities that have successfully found the balance between science and religion will be preserved and survive, which also means a state order based on the smooth coexistence and confession of denominations, History shows that ethnic and religious conflicts can escalate into a state that destroys the foundations of statehood. Creating an enemy based on a different denomination is tantamount to an explosion – first in one country, then in an entire region, until a common civilizational stereotype and clash are created. An example of a successful multi-religious environment is Russia's imperial approach – everyone is free to practice their religion (except for fundamentalist currents) without violating state policy, but on the contrary – successfully creates a state model that can serve as an example to the rest of the world.

The change in the world security architecture cannot happen without the gradual change of one of the main driving forces of the world – money. Over the past ten years, an attempt has been made to de-dollarize the systems among the countries that form the basis of the new architecture – Russia and China. De-dollarization is possible only on two pillars – gold and a new currency, which can be an alternative and coexist with the US dollar. Within ten years, Russian and Chinese gold reserves increase from 400 to 4,000 tons of gold. The strong dollar essentially inflicts all heavy damage on the Russian ruble, but also on the Chinese yuan, the Turkish lira and the Iranian rial. All these countries participate in one of the first three levels of the new security architecture, and on this basis, the change is justified. Most economies in the world are pegged to the US currency because of their national debt denominated in dollars, which makes them highly dependent on changes in interest rates. It was one of the reasons back in 2017, Russia to halve its US foreign debt holdings, but also to arrange bilateral deals with China in rubles or yuan. Again, the means that can protect a country or a circle of countries from creating a bubble and bursting it is to return to the gold standard. Unlike currency, gold always has value and cannot be just paper without value in it. After the end of the First World War, European gold created conditions for future American hegemony and turned dependence on a US creditor into their debtor. Today, this is one of the few real reasons for a sense of security in major European countries – their gold reserves. Germany, Italy and France are the three countries after the United States with the largest gold holdings. Germany with more than 3300 tons, Italy and France with about 2500 tons each, followed by Russia in the world five, thanks to the already mentioned policy of buying and storing gold. The latter is very likely to be among the three wealthiest countries in gold reserves in the next five years. From this point of view, the possibility for a country like Russia to start working in favour of the European currency – the euro – in order to build a counterweight to the dollar should not be underestimated. In the field of wider probabilities discussed in public discourse is the possibility of inventing a new currency, mixing Russian and Chinese under the new name Ruan, which has been repeatedly spoken in public in recent years. Such a scenario from the long-term perspective and the possibility of a confrontation between the current strategic partners seems unlikely.

Within the new security architecture, the true American heritage stands out, which is the result of American power from the time between the end of World War II and the first years of the 21st century. The widespread use of English as a form of collective and most widely used language to exchange data, knowledge and culture. The process of spreading the linguistic and cultural influence described in the previous chapters finds its end and culmination in the time in which the generations grow and live, bred with the American culture. Without re-evaluating it – whether it is positive or negative, but it will certainly take part in the future, which does not belong to the United States alone, but will create a new syncretic culture and world community. If we can talk about American greatness while abstracting from consumer culture, it lies precisely in the spread of the English language and the creation of conditions for it to be called a World common language. If the focus is on the next 20-30 years, there is one sure constant – even then, regardless of the cultural manifestations, the influence of the English language will still be enormous, determining its character as global. History will once again show that the greatness of civilizations does not belong to the strength of their swords or the size of their armies, but the language and spirituality they create and leave as a legacy to the world. Of course, with the significant feature that, after all, this cannot happen without the common state power, which gives way through the means of force.

The world's entry into a new stage in developing international relations, with new security architecture, is a natural process that began about ten years ago. The role of the viral pandemic in 2020 plays the role of catalyst, but not the reason. It was the last straw that filled the glass or the necessary push before a big jump. Its contradictory nature – whether it was a natural process in which the microworld brings balance to the macroworld or a successful social experiment, history will show, but not in the coming years. Only the reactions of states, but also of their leaders, can be analysed in order to achieve some reasonable explanation of both the preparedness of states and the nature of the crisis. However, it is necessary to pay attention to the hypothetical possibility of using new paramilitary methods in the future to bring chaos to the world and afterwards take benefits of it from a given entity or group. In the present case from 2020, it cannot be assumed that the so-called COVID-19 virus is the only reason for redistributing capital, markets and power. As has been noted many times – several processes have already been extremely developed at the end of the ongoing change. But assuming the hypothetical possibility that a pandemic is a conscious act of human design, it is reasonable to be concluded that this is a preliminary test of the system. An attempt for watching how each country, its elite and leaders react in a state of mass panic – at the economic, health and social levels, but especially the last three influenced by the mass information campaign. It, in essence, is the real biological weapon – a virus plus a mass information campaign is equal to mass fear and mass control without firing a single bullet. In this sense, the only societies and elites that manage to control themselves in a very short time are the Chinese, the Russian, partly the US elite, the societies of the Scandinavian countries and isolated examples from Northern Europe. The societies of both Koreas should not be missed – North Korea has taken preventive measures before all others since January 2020, reacting quickly due to the authoritarian nature of its government. It is one of the reasons why it is placed on the third floor of the three-dimensional security architecture – the successful defence of its state and civilization model. Successfully preserving yourself when almost all the rest of the world is trying to change you is the greatest condition for success. Despite its formal democratic character, South Korea has the same spirit and sense of order and discipline, which is why dealing well with a crisis could be anticipated. All other societies and countries have shown that they are unstable as a collective mentality, with an extremely dependent media environment, regardless of official statistics on freedom of speech, etc. and therefore – can be the subject of a successful social experiment in the context of the use of biological and information weapons. The EU's response time can be compared to Churchill's popular aphorism that a lie has travelled half of the world before the truth has a chance to put on its pants. The focus is on slow reactions, not comparing the EU and the "truth". Such a comparison would be hypocritical and misleading.

The good outcome of all the processes described so far, in combination with the pandemic of 2020, would be the lessons to be learned, the messages – to be understood, embedded in the collective consciousness and memory, which would lead to a real change in thinking and action. As for the EU, which in practice, for a month, show that it does not exist as a union, but also the United States, where there is a considerable contrast – while the citizens of New York were in distress, these in Miami continued to go to the beach. It showed that societies are more likely to try to return to the old status quo. However, the fact is that the world is no longer the same – truly strong countries and nations have learned their lessons. Italy will not forget the attitude of the EU; for its part, the EU will not forget the attitude of the United States, and countries like China and Russia have shown that in conditions of a common threat, the competitor and the enemy are helped. They show that personal interests can coexist with universal values, which is the true nature of universalism. The world has been in a state of information warfare for some time. If another physical or biological world war is not allowed to happen, the next decades will pass through the balance of power built within the new three-dimensional security architecture.

Conclusion

The world has yet to accept and adapt to a new state of both existences and as parameters of security in a new framework. A good, lasting peace is possible if the lesson of history is accepted that the order imposed by force, without a social contract, cannot survive in time. With the end of the Cold War, the world was ruled by the sole rule of a country that declared itself exceptional. During this period, the world functions without a consensus and without reaching a signed general agreement to regulate the structure and relations. One of the advantages of the Cold War was its clarity and visible framework – a world operating in a state of bipolar opposition, with clear boundaries. Returning to the tradition of the old treaties, in which European and world politics operate within specific frameworks, is a prerequisite for the success of the new security architecture. Words, no matter how strong, are forgotten and disappear if they are not transferred to paper, supported by a signature. Reaching a new public contract is one of the conditions for establishing and long-term existence of the latest security architecture. The alternative is the continuation of the example started by the United States with the end of the Cold War and the creation of the preconditions for the chaos in the world to continue. The only logic for such a move is the convenience of chaos, of "muddy water", in which there are no rules, and everything is allowed.

Based on such a social contract, the framework of humanity's long-term challenges can be outlined, following the limitation of nuclear weapons. The world is steadily in an age of unconventional wars and problems. It is no longer necessary to go army against army, but on the contrary – use of an invisible enemy – biological weapons, information weapons, etc. At the official level, a form of regulation must be found. But it is equally important what the official position will be – whether a decision will be made to ban scientific experiments because of fear of possible consequences. In a world where advances in technology are making historical time faster than ever, the leaders will be those countries that are the first to make a scientific breakthrough in several areas:

- The creation of artificial intelligence, possessing the "particle of God" – the consciousness and emotions closest to those of a human. Recent years have shown that all countries that claim to be involved in solving world problems invest vast amounts of money in developing an increasingly human-like artificial intelligence. One that can replace its prototype in various activities and situations, from routine household tasks to military missions.

- A breakthrough in genetic modification, which would allow the creation of the "perfect human". The centuries-old human dream of the so-called philosopher's stone, in fact, is not an alchemical delusion but a real opportunity for science. The creation of a person, beyond the accepted natural order, to live even longer, not to get sick, etc. it can be not only a scientific achievement but also a danger.

- The considerable challenge of the near future is to change the sense of reality. The world of technology has allowed a person to be an active participant and creator in the virtual space of the Internet, where the only condition is the payment of the entrance fee. The feeling of freedom that alternative reality offers, which will deepen in detail and sensations, is a real challenge. The individual will be faced with the choice of being overwhelmed by physical reality and the vast flow of information or of being a free prisoner in the world of cyberspace.

- The mastery of space: In 2019,the United States officially established the Space Force as an independent new eighth branch of the army, and Russia's space forces have existed since before. The space race is not a process of the past, on the contrary. From the human nature of curiosity to predatory instincts for submission, this unattainable for now dream of colonization of Space is born. If until two or three decades ago such challenges have been in the field of science fiction, today they are an obsessive ambition and an attempt to realize them. The gaze directed to the stars is probably the most ancient interest and attraction of people.

All these challenges facing societies and countries will continue to develop. The question is whether they will be formally regulated – first in terms of admissibility. If banned, they will undoubtedly continue to exist unofficially. Second, the international debate on "Is it right?Is it moral?" also will not stop. Only putting it in a clear framework, as a part of a new social security treaty in the world, can show the world's readiness to tackle its own ambition.

High technology, scientific breakthroughs and space ambitions are in stark contrast to the world of the little man or the hungry man. The proof that the idea of equality is a necessary dream, while instinct creates contrasts. The world of contrasts will continue to be the world of the future. Nevertheless, the challenges of the recent past and present make it possible to establish an order that creates the conditions for a relatively peaceful existence, with the clear idea that opposition is part of human nature.